Nonprofit Stewardship

A Better Way to Lead Your Mission-Based Organization

Peter C. Brinckerhoff

FIELDSTONE
ALLIANCE

SAINT PAUL
MINNESOTA

We thank The David and Lucile Packard Foundation and the Amherst H. Wilder Foundation for support of this publication.

Fieldstone Alliance is committed to strengthening the performance of the nonprofit sector. Through the synergy of its consulting, training, publishing, and research and demonstration projects, Fieldstone Alliance provides solutions to issues facing nonprofits, funders, and the communities they serve. Fieldstone Alliance was formerly Wilder Publishing and Wilder Consulting departments of the Amherst H. Wilder Foundation. If you would like more information about Fieldstone Alliance and our services, please contact

Fieldstone Alliance
60 Plato Boulevard East, Suite 150
Saint Paul, MN 55107

800-274-6024
www.FieldstoneAlliance.org

Manufactured in the United States of America
Second printing, November 2006

Edited by Vincent Hyman
Text designed by Kirsten Nielsen
Cover designed by Rebecca Andrews
Cover illustration by Tomek Olbinski—
    Images.com. Copyright Images.com

Library of Congress Cataloging-in-Publication Data

Brinckerhoff, Peter C., 1952-
  Nonprofit stewardship : a better way to lead your mission-based organization / Peter C. Brinckerhoff.--
1st ed.
      p. cm.
  Includes bibliographical references and index.
  ISBN 13: 978-0-940069-42-8 (pbk.)
  ISBN 10: 0-940069-42-3 (pbk.)
  1. Leadership. 2. Nonprofit organizations--
Management. I. Title.
  HD57.7.B7447 2004
  658.4'092--dc22
                            2004016369

Printed on recycled paper
10% post-consumer waste

For Bob and Nancy Follett

Great friends, invaluable mentors, tireless community volunteers. Your lives are shining examples of what stewardship really means.

ACKNOWLEDGMENTS

Few, if any, books—at least those of nonfiction—are solely the result of the author's effort. Certainly that is the case here, and I need to thank some people. First, kudos go to the staff and board members of the organizations I have been privileged to work with over the past twenty years. Their examples of selflessness have inspired me on countless occasions.

In appreciation for many great discussions about the nonprofit sector that helped focus my thinking (and kept me off some shaky ground), I thank Heather Iliff of the Alliance for Nonprofits and Don Haider of the Kellogg School of Management at Northwestern University. I look forward to many more such conversations with both of you.

For putting up with me in my often frantic efforts to meet the unreasonable writing deadlines that I set for myself, apologies and love to my wife, Chris, and daughter, Caitlin, our youngest child and the only one of our three not at college when this was written, edited, and finalized.

Finally, many, many thanks to Vince Hyman at Fieldstone Alliance. This was my first time working with Vince, and he is primarily responsible if you find this book useful and readable. I look forward to more collaboration with Vince and Fieldstone Alliance.

Thanks to all.

ABOUT THE AUTHOR

Peter Brinckerhoff is an internationally known expert at helping not-for-profits get more mission for their money. Since embarking on his consulting career by forming his firm, Corporate Alternatives, Inc., in 1982, Peter has worked with thousands of not-for-profit staff and board members throughout the United States. He is a widely published author with more than fifty articles on not-for-profit management in such prominent journals as *Nonprofit World*, *Advancing Philanthropy*, *Contributions*, *Strategic Governance*, and the *Journal of Nonprofit and Voluntary Sector Marketing*. Peter is also the author of the award-winning Mission-Based Management series, which includes the books *Mission-Based Management*, *Financial Empowerment*, *Social Entrepreneurship*, *Faith-Based Management*, and the *Mission-Based Management* and *Mission-Based Marketing Workbooks*. Peter's texts are used in graduate and undergraduate nonprofit programs at more than seventy colleges and universities worldwide.

Peter brings a wide range of practical, hands-on experience to his writing, consulting, and training. He has served as a board member, staff member, and executive director of a number of local, state, and national not-for-profits, and understands all three of these perspectives and their importance in the not-for-profit mix.

Peter received his bachelor's degree from the University of Pennsylvania and his master's in Public Health from the Tulane University School of Public Health. Raised in Connecticut, Peter has lived with his family in Springfield, Illinois, since 1978.

Peter can be reached online through his web site: www.missionbased.com.

CONTENTS

PART I: Understanding Stewardship

PART II: Implementing Stewardship

INTRODUCTION # The New Environment for Not-for-Profits

M ore demand for services. Too few resources to adequately meet that demand. A community that doesn't "get" what you do. A staff that is dedicated but unsure of the future, and certainly underpaid. Higher staff turnover. A board that admires and trusts the staff but comes unprepared to work at meetings and produces decisions of inconsistent quality. Increasing oversight from funders who do not understand that indirect costs are still real costs. Higher expectations for quality of services. Mandates without money. More competition for donated dollars.

If any of these dilemmas sound close to home, join the club. Most not-for-profits would pick at least eight or nine of the issues listed above as *their* issues. Indeed, these concerns reflect most not-for-profits' challenges in the early twenty-first century.

Lester Salamon, in his book *The State of Nonprofit America*, notes that "a conservative estimate puts the total number of 501(c)(3) and 501(c)(4) organizations at 1.2 million, including 350,000 religious congregations in the mid-1990s."[1] Competition has become the norm rather than the exception for not-for-profit organizations. For example, 60 percent of home healthcare workers were employed by not-for-profits in 1982. By 1997, it had dropped to 28 percent. Where were the other employees? No doubt many had migrated to for-profit home healthcare providers.

[1] Lester M. Salamon, *The State of Nonprofit America* (Washington, DC: Brookings Institution Press, 2002), 7, 15, 20.

The same kind of change occurred across the entire human service field over the past fifteen years. Funders have also encouraged competition—either directly, by seeking competitive bids, or indirectly, by encouraging consumer choice among service providers.

At the same time, public attitudes about not-for-profits have suffered from scandals. For example, according to Salamon, in 1999 "only 10 percent [of the public] were willing to agree 'strongly' that most charities are 'honest and ethical in their use of donated funds.'" Other survey data quoted by Salamon shows that in 1996 only 37 percent of respondents felt a great deal of confidence in not-for-profit human service agencies. Not-for-profit leaders have lost the trust of funders and, worse, the confidence of the communities they work for.

More competition and less trust put pressure on not-for-profit decision makers to increase the mission capability of the organization that they steward. Hence this book.

Who This Book Is For

This book is written for the *leaders* of not-for-profit organizations: the supervisory and management staff and governing volunteers (boards of directors).

There are many texts aimed at leaders in general, and some texts especially for not-for-profit leaders. This book is different. It starts from the premise that not-for-profit leaders are *stewards* of the resources that a community entrusts to their organizations. Thus the actions, words, and decisions that not-for-profit leaders do, speak, and make need to be in the context of *stewardship*.

Throughout these pages, you will find my passionately held belief that leading is not enough. Good, but not enough. Important, but inadequate to the challenges you face. This book will show you why *stewardship* is a better model for you, your organization and, most importantly, the people you serve.

The stewardship philosophy presented in this book applies to all types of organizations: direct service providers, associations, groups focusing on the arts, faith, human services, environmental protection, animal welfare, education, poverty, community development, or any of the dozens of other good works that 501(c) organizations provide.

A second audience consists of the donors, grantmakers, government agencies, and others who fund the work of not-for-profit organizations. These have a key stewardship role to play as well.

To get the most from this book, read it as a team of board and staff. The more people who understand the tenets of stewardship and ways to implement it, the better. Team reading increases the likelihood that the ideas in this book will be implemented.

> To get the most from this book, read it as a team of board and staff. Team reading increases the likelihood that the ideas in this book will be implemented.

This Book's Promise to You

The stewardship model of leadership can help your organization improve its mission capability. Being a steward of your organization forces you to keep your organization's mission foremost—and helps you make decisions that are best for the people your organization serves. In other words, *stewardship helps you do more good for more people.*

By reading this book you will learn

- How the concepts of stewardship apply to your role in your organization

- How to view decision making in a way that improves your organization's capacity to achieve its mission

- How to see expending resources as an investment in your organization's mission

- What stewardship roles mean for managers, volunteers, and funders of your organization

- What kind of leader you are now, and how you can improve as a steward

- How to incorporate stewardship into day-to-day management decisions, long-range planning, financial resource allocations, and human resources issues
- How to lead as a steward in times of growth and in times of crisis, and how to grow other stewards in your organization

How to Use This Book

This book is full of ideas to use right away. Dozens of real-world examples help make this book practical—look for the **For Example** tag to find them. Specific applications of stewardship concepts are presented in the **Hands-On** sidebars that appear throughout this book. At the end of each chapter is a list of **Discussion Questions** that focus on the key points of the chapter. These questions are designed to reinforce the ideas brought up in the chapter and, more importantly, to generate discussion among the people reading it together.

This book has two parts. Part I includes the first two chapters, which focus on the philosophy and tenets of stewardship. These chapters contain the big concepts but also include many examples and hands-on ideas that you can start to use quickly. Part II explores more specific applications of stewardship, including how stewardship ideas apply to planning, finance, and crisis management. There's also a set of assessment tools that helps the organization's leaders look at their stewardship as a group, and also look at their personal level of stewardship.

Let's look at the chapters in more detail.

Part I: Understanding Stewardship

Chapter 1: Stewardship: A New Way of Thinking. Chapter 1 provides the philosophical basis for the rest of this book. It describes the eight characteristics of a mission-based steward and provides your first opportunity to weigh yourself against these characteristics. It explains the various stewardship roles that exist in your not-for-profit and why these roles are essential in a well-balanced organization. This chapter also discusses the "three truths of not-for-profits" and how they fit with the model of stewardship. It also takes a brief look at nine characteristics of successful not-for-profits—qualities good stewards will want to see in their own organizations. Finally, this chapter looks at why successful organizational stewardship is a team effort and how you can include your staff and volunteers in the stewardship model.

Chapter 2: How Stewards Make Decisions. Chapter 2 begins to look at stewardship in some detail. It shows you why the stewardship framework is applicable to mission-based organizations, and why stewards work hard to improve their organization's mission capabilities. It discusses the concept of dual return on investment, the meaning of the mantra "It's not your organization," how to focus consistently on mission, and how to value your staff more. This chapter also provides you with useful decision-making tools. These decision tools can be used for decisions major or minor. Finally, this chapter looks at ways to find and use the skills of people outside your organization to make better decisions.

Part II: Implementing Stewardship

Chapter 3: Board Stewardship. Board, staff, and funders are all intertwined in the operations of a not-for-profit. Chapter 3 examines the first of the three distinct, yet interwoven, stewardship roles—the governing volunteers or board of directors. It outlines how board stewards should look at their duties and how they can make better stewardship decisions. It also examines some individual board roles including the president, the treasurer, and the board as fundraisers. Finally, this chapter discusses the important issue of managing board liability.

Chapter 4: Staff and Volunteer Stewardship. Chapter 4 looks at the next stewardship role—paid employees and those dedicated volunteers who also serve staff-like functions. Like Chapter 3, this chapter starts with an overall look at how good staff stewards view their responsibilities and how they can make better decisions. Then it examines the duties of some specific staff members including the chief executive officer, the chief financial officer, the management team, other staff, and volunteers.

Chapter 5: Funders as Stewards. Funders provide much of the money used by the not-for-profit sector. Chapter 5 discusses why funders can and should be stewards not only of their own funds, but also of their grantees' resource allocation methods. This chapter looks specifically at the roles of contractors, donors, and grantors, and makes recommendations for changes in the relationship between funders and not-for-profit organizations.

Chapter 6: Planning Your Path. This chapter shows you how to plan for your organization's future, which really means focusing its resources where they can do the most good for the most people. It also reveals goals that nearly all not-for-profits should consider, and some outcome measurement tools that you can use to assess your organization's progress. Finally, this chapter details a planning process that can engage the entire community in the strategic planning process.

Chapter 7: Financial Stewardship. The first rule of not-for-profits is Mission, mission, and more mission. The second rule of not-for-profits is No money, no mission. Chapter 7 looks at specific ways to keep enough money available to do your mission work, and some new stewardship-rich ways of viewing your finances, your budgeting, and your financial reporting. This chapter also covers the important issue of dual return on investment and gives you some pointers on saving, borrowing, and investing your funds. It shows you ways to make your organization more financially transparent and ways to protect the assets your organization has worked so hard to attain.

Chapter 8: Taking Good Risk. Stewards look at reasonable risk as good, but how do you know what's "reasonable" for your organization? This chapter will review some ways your organization can develop a risk-taking culture that improves its mission delivery. It examines the concept of social entrepreneurship and shows you how your stewardship decision-making model fits with the ideas of risk and the dual return on investment.

Chapter 9: Stewardship in Good Times and Bad. Is it really easier to lead in good times as opposed to bad? Perhaps. But both growth and cutbacks have their unique challenges. Chapter 9 looks at special stewardship skills to apply in these situations as well as some crisis management tools that really work.

Chapter 10: Taking Stock of Stewardship. After all the suggestions and ideas presented in Chapters 1 through 9, you will understand stewardship and how to incorporate it into your organization's culture. But where do you stand now? What's your starting point? This chapter provides you with a stewardship self-assessment, one that you can use as a starting point now and, later, as a reference point to measure your progress. This chapter also uncovers signs of trouble for any not-for-profit organization.

Resources. Finally, this book includes a list of resources for further study and exploration by you and your staff. These include print, periodical, software, and web resources. If you are a lifelong learner, this chapter will help.

Recap

Not-for-profit leaders are *stewards* of the resources that a community entrusts to their organizations. To survive in an environment of competition and scrutiny, not-for-profit organizations require strong mission-based stewardship. This book is written for the leaders of your organization and is designed to be read as a group. You can move ahead quickly by reading the brief chapter descriptions and selecting the chapters that are most important to your organization.

I passionately believe that the principles and practices included here can help you unleash improved mission capability. Stewardship, at its core, has two huge benefits for you and your organization: First, it's the *smart* thing to do because it works. More importantly, it's the *right* thing to do and, as such, it should fit in with your organization's mission focus and set of values. Most of us work for not-for-profit organization out of a desire to help others. The stewardship model of leadership can help you do more good for more people, and feel better about yourself at the same time.

PART I

Understanding Stewardship

CHAPTER ONE # Stewardship: A New Way of Thinking

I f you are like most not-for-profit staff and governing volunteers, you signed on to do good
works. Your organization serves others: perhaps individuals, your local
community, your state, the nation, or the entire world. In other words the
end product of your organization is not about self-aggrandizement, it's
about mission, serving others. So it shouldn't be a stretch to look at the
organization you work with as a vehicle to help others.

The stewardship philosophy of leadership goes a step further. It reminds
us that in the not-for-profit sector organizations actually *belong* to the
communities they serve, and leaders have temporary stewardship over
their assets.

The key concept here is this: as a steward, your job is to manage your not-
for-profit with the same care, the same attention to detail, the same level
of responsibility that you would give to someone else's property—because
that's the reality. "Your" not-for-profit is not, in actuality, yours; it really
belongs to the community and you are but the temporary steward of its
resources. While many of us take justifiable pride in "our" organization,
"our" staff, "our" board, and of course "our" mission, in far too many cases
"our" becomes "my" in more ways than just as a descriptor, and soon the
organization loses its mission-first focus.

This concept takes some getting used to, because we have so much of ourselves wrapped up in our work. Realizing that you are a manager of someone else's resources is the first step, and a hard one, toward becoming a steward. Yet it is a fact based on the legal structure of a 501(c)(3). With that in mind, here is a definition of a mission-based steward:

> *A mission-based steward is a person who consistently leads the organization in managing the resources of the community in a manner that maximizes its mission-effectiveness.*

This definition will get us started and will be the basis of everything we look at throughout the book. In all of your decision making, in all of your planning, in every resource allocation choice you make, you'll come back to this definition and ask yourself, "Am I making the choice that best enhances our mission? Am I offering the community the best outcome for their investment in us?" We'll spend a lot of time on this in the coming pages, but start thinking about this now.

The Characteristics of a Mission-Based Steward

Many people directly connect their own career choice to a particular teacher who made a subject "come alive" for them. When a teacher's skill, subject knowledge, and enthusiasm all combine, the learning experience can be fabulous, even life-changing.

So it is for leadership. Success is more than book knowledge, managerial skill, or the ability to plan, budget, and delegate. A successful leader, a true steward, has a group of very special characteristics that work together for the benefit of their organization and its mission. These characteristics are remarkably consistent, whether the steward is a member of the executive team, a line supervisor, or a governing volunteer.

Stewardship Roles Throughout the Organization

Everyone has a role in stewarding the resources the not-for-profit has been entrusted with. Here's what each class of steward needs to consider.

Board of directors

The board has five stewardship roles. The first four are standard to most books on not-for-profit boards: 1) to provide policy oversight for the organization; 2) to plan for the future; 3) to advocate for the organization in the community; 4) to raise funds. The fifth role is new: to coach, support, and remind the staff about stewardship as a philosophy, and to bring that passion for stewardship outside the walls of the organization as community networkers and fundraisers.

Staff

Staff are stewards as well—starting with the executive and running right to the line staff. All staff should embody stewardship in their regular interactions with each other, the board, the community, and most importantly, with the people they serve. Staff stewards consistently remind themselves and each other that "It's not our stuff, so let's do better."

Nongoverning volunteers

Nongoverning volunteers are crucial to many organizations. These wonderful people give of their time and talents, but should never assume that they are not responsible for the mission and the resources of the organization. Nongoverning volunteers may in fact provide mission directly (delivering meals on wheels, being museum docents or wildlife interpreters) as well as doing clerical chores or raising funds. They, too, need to be imbued with the attitude that "This is about other people and not me. I need to do better every day."

Funders

Funders are in a key stewardship position. Obviously, they provide money for certain services and activities. They also oversee the expenditure of these funds and the provision of services. Here, however, is the key: funders should do this in a balanced way, letting the board and staff run the organization, not demanding so much accountability that the organization's resources are all spent being accountable rather than doing mission.

The not-for-profit steward has the following qualities:

1. Balance
2. Humility
3. Accountability
4. Integrity
5. The ability to motivate
6. A thirst for innovation
7. Communication skills
8. A quest for lifelong learning

Let's look at each characteristic in some more depth:

1. Balance

A steward must balance a variety of competing priorities. These include mission and money, staff and board, needs and wants, and work and play.

There is no greater challenge than trying to balance the ever-present competition between **mission and money**. "Mission first," but "No money, no mission." A successful steward understands that even though it hurts to say no to some service requests, the people the organization serves will benefit most, and for the longest period of time, if it sticks to what it does well—its core competencies.

A second challenge is that of balancing **staff and board**. Good stewards develop trust with both so that when the priorities of staff and board differ, resolutions can be made that don't injure the organization. Stewards also work to keep both groups strong, informed, and well educated. If the board is strong and the staff is weak, or vice versa, the organization gets out of balance.

The third area of balance for a good steward is making sure that the organization balances community **needs and wants**. People have needs, but they seek wants. Not-for-profit organizations need to *give people what they need in a way that they will want*. This is the essence of mission-based marketing, and for a steward to ignore this fact is to imperil the organization. Working to meet wants is harder than just giving people what they need. It requires diligence in developing a systematic way of asking the people served what they want.

The fourth area of balance for a steward is that of **work and play** (also work and rest). As a steward, you have great responsibilities, and many people depend on you. It is too easy to focus on work at the expense of your own mental, physical, or family health. A good not-for-profit steward must also be a good steward of his or her own body, and must lead others in the organization to be the same.

2. Humility

Most of us take pride in our roles. This is especially true for those on the senior management team or board of directors, and so this section is especially addressed to you if you are part of that group. You should be proud of your accomplishments—but not pride filled. Pride can creep into management styles and result in a "my way or the highway" organization, one that is centered around a person rather than the mission.

Good stewards are humble about their role in the organization, for good reason. First, as already discussed, it's not their stuff. The resources that they manage belong to others. Once they understand that while they may be the head steward, they are not the owner, everything else flows pretty easily.

Second, stewards realize that the management of the organization is really a support function; managers are really there to support line staff. This philosophy is often called bottom-up management, and it literally turns the organizational chart on its head, with the line staff at the top and the senior management at the bottom. It's the right thing to do and it's the smart thing to do, but it's humbling as well.

If you believe in bottom-up management, then you have to remember two more things. First, when things go right, your staff get the credit, and when things go wrong, you get the blame. This is the role of a leader,

Practical Applications of the Eight Stewardship Characteristics

There are many ways to apply the eight stewardship characteristics. The following examples should get you started.

Balance. There are a thousand ways to seek balance. Here is one for balancing work and play: if you don't regularly exercise, start—even with just a ten-minute walk a day. Organize a walking group at work, and spend half of your lunch break walking. Bring in speakers on nutrition, preventive health, and so forth. Sponsor diet and nutrition groups, hold before- or after-work yoga sessions on site, reward staff for weight loss, co-pay health club dues. Let your staff see you take time for your health and time for your family. There is very compelling data that healthy people work harder while they are at work, and miss less time for illness and stress than those who aren't.

Humility. Here's a humble approach to communication: It doesn't matter what you say, it matters what they hear. It doesn't matter what you write, it matters what they read. In practice, this means that when you communicate with others, you must drop your pride about what you've said. If they misunderstand you, it is your humble job to figure out why and restate your message until you're sure they do understand.

Accountability. Are you open to suggestions, corrections, and criticism from your peers and your employees? Does everyone in the organization get a written and oral performance review at least annually? Are those reviews two-way, with supervisors evaluated by their employees? Do you have a "fix the blame" culture rather than a "fix the problem" culture? Do you have a strategic and annual plan that people actually use as a management tool? All of these ideas and actions create a culture of accountability, critical for a stewardship organization.

Integrity. Look at your practices to see if you "walk the talk." If your organization's values statement declares that "We value the dignity of every individual" and yet you discipline people by yelling at them in public, you've missed the boat. If the rules state that everyone needs to be in the office by eight o'clock and you come in at nine, it's time to reset your alarm. If everyone has to learn a new communications software, you'd better be first in line for training. Same for dress code, reimbursement, accountability, evaluation—you name it.

The ability to motivate. Motivation starts with walking the talk. What you say matters, but what you do matters more. Motivation also has a component of balance: you need to know when to lead the rah-rah cheer, and when to be quiet and let things happen. It also requires knowing the people you need to motivate. Constant cheerleading turns some people off, others need it, and others want a small quiet pat on the back. Everyone is different—so listen, ask, observe, and motivate selectively.

A thirst for innovation. Look at your policies and practices to uncover how you value innovation in your culture. For example, do your performance evaluation criteria ask, "What new innovation, idea, process, method, or improvement did (the person) contribute to our mission in the past year?" You can build an innovative culture by making innovation an expectation—and rewarding it when it happens.

Communication skills. This requires a willingness to learn, re-learn, and practice. The ability to communicate is not an inherited skill, whether you are expressing your passion for your organization's mission or motivating staff to complete a certain task in a certain way by a certain time. It is a learned one, and learned skills need to be reviewed, refreshed, and practiced.

A quest for lifelong learning. First, add criteria in your staff evaluation process that deal with continuing education, and add them to everyone's goals at each evaluation. Second, if you don't already have one, assemble a staff development team that looks at all your training needs, including those mandated by funders or local regulations (such fire drills, disaster drills, and CPR refresher courses). Beyond that, what kinds of training would your staff like, and what can you provide? If resources are an issue, there are numerous no- and low-cost options available.

particularly if he or she wants a staff with high morale. Again, this is the right thing to do as well as the smart thing to do—and certainly a humbling thing to do.

3. Accountability

Who are not-for-profit stewards accountable to? Or perhaps the better question is, who should stewards be accountable to? The answer is humbling: to their board of directors, their staff, their community, the people the organization serves, their funders, and, of course, to themselves. Accountability translates into several behaviors—seeking feedback, and seeking a level of personal acceptance that balances over-accountability and under-accountability.

As a steward, seek feedback on your own performance, so you can improve it. Thus if you are the executive, make sure the board evaluates you annually. If you evaluate your staff, make sure they evaluate your supervision as well. Similarly, make sure your organization seeks input by asking, surveying, interviewing, and holding focus groups with the community whose resources you steward. In other words, help the community hold you (personally) and the rest of the organization accountable. These steps to hold yourself accountable will help you when you hold your staff accountable (see Integrity on page 11).

Accountability is a spectrum. In the nonprofit sector some leaders tend to be over-accountable—to take on an inhuman level of responsibility. Many are the leaders who feel personally responsible for the hunger in their community, for example, or who can't sleep soundly because they know there are homeless individuals left outside on a frigid night. This is, of course, a short road to ulcers and an emotional breakdown. Oddly enough, a certain degree of acceptance of the human condition can help the overachieving steward reach a more balanced accountability. Acceptance certainly does not mean settling for the status quo: the organization's mission is to improve things, not to march in place. But acceptance helps stewards strike a balance, doing what they can, doing it well, and accepting that they *can't fix everything*. Overachieving leaders need to accept that they worked as hard as they could today, yesterday, and last week. Finally, such stewards can balance their hyper-accountability with a little humility. Just as no one person can claim credit for every success, no one can claim credit for every failure!

On the other end of the spectrum are those people who try to duck responsibility. Such leaders need to enter and stay in a no-whining zone. Accountable people don't whine (or at least they keep it to a minimum). For example, if you've a tendency to complain, don't whine about workload, since it is mostly through choices—the organization's or your own—that such work is accumulated. Don't whine about regulations or audits or paperwork: these are all a cost of doing business. Finally, don't whine because whining has nothing to do with your mission. Stewards who lead in this area will find that the rest of their staff are much more likely to follow.

4. Integrity

Good leaders lead by example. In formal terms, a steward embodies the values of the organization in his or her actions. Put in more colloquial terms, a steward walks the talk. As a leader of a not-for-profit you are carefully observed, both inside and outside the organization. Your actions speak for you.

In management and leadership terms, actions can negate a whole lot of words. What you say matters, but what you do matters more.

> FOR EXAMPLE: Early in the German occupation of Denmark during World War II, the Germans declared that throughout Denmark all Jews had to wear a gold star on their clothes. The next morning the Danish king, who was not a Jew, went out for his daily horseback ride through the streets of Copenhagen with a gold star clearly visible on his sleeve. Thousands of Danes followed his example at no small risk. He didn't have to protest or rant against the Germans. His actions spoke volumes.

Lead by example. What you *say* matters. What you *do* matters *more*.

5. The ability to motivate

Mission effectiveness, the goal of a steward, is nearly impossible without an inspired, motivated board and staff. And thus successful stewards have the ability to motivate others, to get them to go beyond the adequate to the excellent, to help them overcome obstacles, set high goals, strive to be the best at their chosen craft.

You can't motivate your people without knowing them. Just as people learn in different styles, they are encouraged and motivated differently. Some people love "rah-rah"; some are completely turned off by it. For some people a quiet pat on the back once a month is enough; others really, really need to have their picture in the "Employee of the Month" frame in the lobby. To motivate selectively you first have to take the time to know your people.

Second, most of us (but not all) are more motivated when we work in teams. It's either the peer approval or the peer pressure, or both, but the work gets done. And teams can provide support in tough personal or organizational situations. Use teams to keep people motivated.

Third, visible leaders motivate people, so lead out front. In the military, the best leaders try to be among the line troops as much as possible, to be seen, to shake hands, to inspire by their attendance as much as their oratory. Get out among your people regularly. Say thanks and ask what you can do to help them.

Finally, remember to value your line staff and show them respect. The people who work with you want the same things you do: to have a meaningful job, to be treated with respect, to be told the truth, to be challenged. Treat others the way you would like them to treat you.

6. A thirst for innovation

Innovation is the engine of improvement. Stewards seek to maximize mission-effectiveness. Stewardship organizations are constantly trying new things, accepting that not all experiments work, but trying again nonetheless. A steward also models innovation, stretching personally while encouraging others to do so. If you hear yourself saying things like "We all need to be available to our funders, board, and others by e-mail and voice mail," and then in the same breath telling people that you won't be using e-mail since you "don't like computers," are you modeling innovation?

The most innovative organizations usually try to avoid wholesale change in favor of continuous small improvements. The Japanese caution against trying to improve 100 percent at a time, as people will resist. Rather, they seek to improve 1 percent a day—every day.

7. Communication skills

There is no question that a leader must communicate well. You have to be able to communicate your vision, your passion, your goals, and your desired outcomes. You can't delegate effectively without good communications skills. As a steward, you must also communicate your stewardship beliefs and your focus on mission.

Communication includes speaking, writing, body language, and *listening*. You also communicate, as noted above, by your actions. It's not just about "you" talking to "them."

A few points about communication: First, *being a good communicator is not an inherited skill*. It is something you learn, and anything learned needs to be practiced. Second, communication technique is important, but only 50 percent of successful communication is technique; the other 50 percent is based on trust. If the people to whom you talk, write, or present don't trust that you are telling them the truth as you know it, they won't fully listen—they'll sort of listen, and sort of wonder whether they are being conned. So say what you mean and mean what you say. If you promise to get back to a staff person with a decision on a purchase by telling them "I'll get back to you tomorrow on that," you have just given your word that you will, in fact, give them the answer by the close of business tomorrow.

Third, *a crucial communication skill is listening*. Consider the old saying: "No one ever learned anything while they were talking." If you value your

> Only 50 percent of successful communication is technique; the other 50 percent is based on trust.

staff, and if you want them to provide you with their ideas and opinions, you need to listen to them. Remember, there is a big difference between listening and waiting your turn to talk.

8. A quest for lifelong learning

Lifelong learning is a crucial part of stewardship. How can we do the best with our community's resources if we aren't always seeking better ways to use them in pursuit of mission? Lifelong learning is also an expression of several other stewardship characteristics, among them humility ("I'll never know enough") and innovation ("I've got to find ways to do better").

Lifelong learning is an area where you have to lead in both word and deed. First, the organization needs to value continuing education in its budget, in its personnel evaluations, and in its board and staff meetings. You as a steward need to attend training of varying types, and then report what you've learned to others. If there is mandatory training in, say, workplace safety or harassment, you need to attend as much as the people who work for you.

Learning doesn't have to be expensive. For example, you could start a reading group for your management team: pick a book, read a chapter a week, and discuss what you've learned. You can use online courses, the not-for-profit management or certificate program at your local university, corporate training programs, your community foundation, your management support organization, or your state or national trade group. Check out what's there, look at your budget, and set up a program that starts slowly and grows. And always lead by demonstrating your own commitment to lifelong learning.

Now you know the overall characteristics of a mission-based steward. (The sidebar Stewardship Roles Throughout the Organization, page 5, reveals how some of these characteristics play out in specific roles.) Next let's look at nine characteristics of a successful not-for-profit.

Three Truths about Your Not-for-Profit

There are three truths about not-for-profit organizations that underpin this entire book. They are a vital foundation for stewardship, and adopting them as part of your philosophy will make it easier for you to see yourself as a steward and to bring others with you.

1. Your not-for-profit is a mission-based business. Yes, a *business*—but one that puts mission first. A steward's job is to get the most mission with the resources available, and business skills can move your mission forward. Marketing, finance, controls, good human resources, and business development are all essential to a successful mission-based organization. When it behaves as a mission-based business, it is more driven, more focused, more responsive to the people you serve, and more accountable to all stakeholders.

2. No one gives your organization a dime. No one gives you anything. Not the feds, not the states, not the United Way, not the city, county, local foundation, not a corporate donor, or even a private individual. All of the funders listed above don't just send you money, they *want* something—some service provided—for their cash. Thus you *earn* every dime you get. Further, if you earn the money, you aren't "subsidized." Subsidies are what people get for doing nothing. So if your organization has considered itself "subsidized," stop it. *You are paid for the services you deliver.*

3. Being not-for-profit does not demand that you make no profit. One of the most damaging urban legends about the not-for-profit community is that the name of the sector, *nonprofit* or *not-for-profit*, has something to do with the organization's appropriate bottom line. As in, "Well, you're a nonprofit, so you shouldn't make money, shouldn't charge me, shouldn't have two dimes to rub together at the end of the fiscal year." You've heard it all before, and may believe it yourself at some level.

Well, here's the truth. It is absolutely legal for your organization to make money, and *as a not-for-profit steward, you have to look at profit as a good thing.* If you want to grow, want to serve more people, want to innovate and try new things, you need to make money. Of course, not everything you do can or should earn a profit. Profit isn't the point, it is just a strategy for accomplishing your mission. Treat it as such.

You'll see these three truths play out in many ways throughout this book.

HANDS-ON

What Stewards Strive For:
Nine Characteristics of a Successful Not-for-Profit

There are a number of characteristics of successful organizations that make them successful stewards, all of which must exist for best use of "other people's stuff." These characteristics are

1. A viable mission
2. A businesslike board
3. A strong, well-educated staff
4. Technological savvy
5. Social entrepreneurism
6. A bias for marketing
7. Financial empowerment
8. A compelling vision
9. Tight controls

Let's look at how each characteristic relates to the stewardship model of leadership. We'll be returning to them as we move through the rest of the book.

1. A viable mission

Your organization exists because of your mission. It continues because of your mission. Most of your board, staff, and volunteers show up most days because of your mission. So that mission needs to be viable—alive in the actions of the staff and board, alive in the understanding of the community and funders.

To achieve that viability, a mission statement needs to be short, easily memorized, and quickly (and often) quoted. Stewardship *requires* that your actions make you more mission capable, and to do that you have to know and understand your mission.

Give Your Mission Statement a Checkup

Want to know if your mission statement is still alive? Give it a checkup with the following questions.

1. Is it current? Has it been carefully reviewed in the past three years? Does it use current terminology for your organization's field?

2. Does it accurately describe what your organization does, the people it serves, and where it does its work?

3. Are you working within the bounds of your mission statement? For example, if you have geographic exclusions ("Helping the homeless in Cook County") and you receive income from other counties, you could well have a problem with Unrelated Business Income Tax, something you really want to pay attention to. The same issue exists with demographic exclusions, which may set limits by ethnicity, economic status, age, and gender, or other features.

4. Is your mission statement short? If, for understandable political reasons, you have to have a long statement, consider shortening the mission, which is supposed to talk about why you are in existence and add a statement of values about how you do the mission (honesty, openness, respect for everyone, and so on). That way, the mission statement can be short enough to recite, but you won't offend anyone from the board, staff, or community who feels deeply about a particular value.

5. Did you file the mission statement (or revised statement) with the Internal Revenue Service if you are a U.S. not-for-profit? Send the IRS a letter including the date of the board meeting when the mission statement was revised, a copy of the old and new statements, a rationale for the revision, and a list of board members voting for and against the revision.

Mission statements are central to your stewardship, so make sure you have the best, most useful, most motivating mission possible.

2. A businesslike board

An executive director or senior manager who is a good steward can't do everything alone. He or she needs others, and the first wave of help should come from the board of directors. Boards need a wide skill set, one that changes over time as the organization's needs evolve.

> **FOR EXAMPLE:** I've been directly or indirectly involved with boards for many years. I've watched one metamorphose numerous times. In 1982, the board, which runs an organization working with people with disabilities, was made up of three or four businesspeople, and the rest were parents of people the group served. As the organization grew, it added a dozen group homes and a sheltered workshop. Thus we needed architects, builders, attorneys, and bankers on the board, and we got them, while still keeping our parent representation. By 1990 the service philosophy had changed, and the board needed to segue into a group with more community links including clergy, community activists, and the like. Finally, with recent funding cuts and a more competitive environment, fundraising has become a key board role. However, parents and family members of those served still represent a significant portion of the board seats, which is essential.

This example illustrates both the need for regular change on the board, as the organization's needs change, and the need for certain skills. The specific skills vary over time and from one organization to the next, but two kinds of people are always needed: advocates and businesspeople.

Advocates are people who passionately believe in the mission of the organization. These people keep you true to the first rule of not-for-profits, which, as you already know, is "Mission, Mission, Mission!"

Businesspeople are individuals who understand cash flow, feasibility studies, budgeting, human resources, and marketing. These people keep you true to the second rule of not-for-profits, which is "No money, no mission!"

These two groups provide a dynamic tension in the board deliberations, which keeps the organization in balance between mission and money—not an easy thing to achieve. In some cases you have a businessperson who is also an advocate. But not always.

Having a board that supports and implements a stewardship mind-set is crucial. We'll talk more about board roles in Chapter 3.

3. A strong, well-educated staff

Staff are at the heart of mission delivery, so it pays to invest in their development. In any field of endeavor, the ongoing advances in service techniques, quality assurance, marketing, finance, and technology are staggering. You can't keep up, and your staff can't keep up, unless you seek continuing education for yourself, your employees, and your volunteers. This is an investment in mission, not an optional expense. To paraphrase the old adage, "Knowledge is better mission." Chapter 4 will deal with staffing issues in some detail, including a management and supervision style for stewards.

4. Technological savvy

Intelligent use of technology can increase productivity, resulting in much better stewardship of the community's resources. You don't need to have the newest equipment, but you do need to be online, and to figure out ways to use all this wonderful technology to move the mission forward. Many organizations still view technology as a luxury. It's not. It's a tool, and an increasingly inexpensive one. It's also an expectation of the community you serve. Lack of technological savvy on your organization's part may translate to real or perceived lack of quality. Wise use of technology to improve mission is good stewardship, not a fad, trend, or waste of money.

5. Social entrepreneurism

A *social entrepreneur* seeks to take reasonable risks for the benefit of the people the organization serves. The connection to stewardship is clear:

risks are taken for other people. Social entrepreneurs understand that risk is a good thing. Innovation—a characteristic of stewards noted above—requires risk. To advance your capability to do good works, you've got to try new methods of delivery. Thus, risk is inherent in improving your mission capability. Social entrepreneurs balance risk with reason by using feasibility studies and business plans, but they don't shy away from the new or the untested. Their stewardship ideals push the organization to higher levels of quality, new ways of service.

6. A bias for marketing

Marketing has tremendous application to mission and to stewardship. Marketing for not-for-profits is not about sales, but about meeting the *needs* of the population the organization serves in a way that also meets their *wants*. If a not-for-profit meets a need in the way that a market wants, it will be more effective, more efficient, and more productive, accomplishing more with the same resources.

Marketing has many applications in a not-for-profit, with implications for staff and board satisfaction, the happiness of funders and, most importantly, the quality of services and satisfaction of the people you serve. Understanding marketing and it implications is also a crucial part of any new service expansion or business development activity you may undertake, and is a crucial part of taking the risks you assess reasonable for your organization.

Finally, marketing is always a team effort. Everyone has to be involved for your organization to be its most successful. It's not just your job.

7. Financial empowerment

Successful mission-based organizations use their financial resources in innovative ways, empowering them to provide more mission. Financial empowerment is not just financial stability, although many readers would probably settle for that right now. Empowerment includes having and growing an endowment, improving the use of your financial reporting, establishing and maintaining adequate cash reserves, establishing an endowment, borrowing appropriately, and, as we discussed in the sidebar Three Truths about Your Not-for-Profit, page 15, making money.

Good management of financial resources is often the first thing people think about when they consider the concept of stewardship, and it is certainly important. Good financial stewardship requires you to make careful decisions regarding return on investment, how you treat human resources, and infrastructure such as facilities and equipment. So financial planning, budgeting, and decision making are very important in the stewardship mix. (More on financial empowerment and financial stewardship in Chapter 7.)

8. A compelling vision

You can't be an effective steward if you don't know where you're going—and that requires a vision and a plan. Planning requires time, research, and lengthy discussion between the board and staff to set priorities, focus resources, and choose goals. Planning also requires that you step back from day-to-day operations and engage in "big think"—generating a compelling vision. Planning allows you to focus your energies and your resources on what your community needs most that you also do best. It gets right to the effectiveness component of good stewardship. More on planning and vision in Chapter 6.

9. Tight controls

For most managers, financial and policy controls are even less fun than planning. After all, aren't they just more paperwork: personnel policies, financial policies, media policies, quality assurance rules, conflict of interest policies, and the like? Developing policies to prevent bad things and encourage good things is certainly the job of a management steward. Both financial controls and policy controls help you reduce the risks you are taking with the community's resources.

These nine characteristics work, but only if they work as a group. Entrepreneurship cannot exist without marketing, vision cannot be realized without finance, either a board or a staff operating without the other is doomed to failure, controls allow for both board and staff to manage rather than administer and, of course, the mission is the basis of it all.

So think of these characteristics as a matched set, or if you like, as an orchestra playing a symphony. When all elements work in concert, the music is rich.

Recap

In this chapter, we've set the stage for everything that will follow. You've learned the definition of a mission-based steward:

> *A mission-based steward is a person who consistently leads the organization in managing the resources of the community in a manner that maximizes its mission-effectiveness.*

Then we looked at eight characteristics of a mission-based steward:

1. Balance
2. Humility
3. Accountability
4. Integrity
5. The ability to motivate
6. A thirst for innovation
7. Communication skills
8. A quest for lifelong learning

In a sidebar, we highlighted three core truths about your not-for-profit:

1. Your not-for-profit is a mission-based business
2. No one gives your organization a dime
3. Being not-for-profit does not demand that you make no profit

We also reviewed nine characteristics of a successful not-for-profit:

1. A viable mission
2. A businesslike board
3. A strong, well-educated staff
4. Technological savvy
5. Social entrepreneurism
6. A bias for marketing
7. Financial empowerment
8. A compelling vision
9. Tight controls

Stewardship starts with you. No matter where you are in your organization you can read this book, get excited, learn some skills, and start from where you are now with your colleagues at work. You can evidence the characteristics of a mission-based steward in your work consistently—even if the rest of the organization is not yet on board.

But the techniques in this book will work better if more people participate—so try to enlist as many of your staff and board as possible on the stewardship train. As noted earlier, read this book as a group, a chapter at a time, and use the discussion questions to learn from each other.

So now the stage is set. You have learned what stewardship means, the criteria for becoming a mission-based steward, and some philosophies about successful organizations.

In the next chapter we'll look at some practical applications of the stewardship concept to day-to-day work.

CHAPTER ONE DISCUSSION QUESTIONS[2]

1. In what ways do we already practice stewardship?

2. Do we really act as though our resources are not ours? How can we get better at this?

3. What do we think about the "three truths" (see page 15): ? Are we really a mission-based business? Do we believe we earn every dollar we take in? Do we strive to capture a profit that we can reinvest in further development?

4. How can we be more humble? Do we value our line staff adequately? Can we do better?

5. What can we do to get our board, funders, and other volunteers to come with us as stewards?

6. How do we involve the rest of the staff?

---

[2] We encourage you to address these questions as a group—and hence the questions are written for group discussion. But if you have no group, substitute "I" for "we."

CHAPTER TWO

How Stewards Make Decisions

All organizations face tough decisions—and certainly the jobs of most organizational leaders revolve around decisions. And so the first and most important application of the stewardship concept is in making decisions. This chapter will provide you with a decision-making tool—one that you will see again later in the book, as the formula can be adopted for various types of decisions. But before we look at that tool, it's important to fully understand what it feels like to "own" the notion that *It's not your organization*. Then we'll look at a corollary to that axiom: Seek maximum yield on your mission investment. Finally, we'll see how these play out when making decisions. By the end of this chapter, you'll be ready to move on to look at specific types of stewardship.

It's Not Your Organization

First and foremost in stewardship is the pursuit of mission, but the manner in which you make that pursuit comes after the realization that "your" organization is not yours—it's the community's, and you have temporary stewardship over the assets. This colors *all* the ideas and suggestions that appear in this book, even in areas such as finance, planning, and risk.

For some people, this application of stewardship is hard; for others it is not a stretch at all. Let's walk through the logic sequence you can use to become comfortable with the idea yourself, as well as help others buy into the stewardship concept.

Most not-for-profit staff, board, and volunteers sign up for the challenge of doing good works, often spurred by personal experience relevant to the organization's mission. Whatever the mission, the organization *serves* others, perhaps individuals, the local community, the state, nation, or entire world. In other words, the end product is not about self-aggrandizement, it's about serving others. This is pretty clear to most people, though some may have trouble following through on it!

But does the organization *belong* to others? Yes, in several ways. First, the board of directors of a 501(c)(3) does not represent stockholders as a for-profit corporate board does. The board represents *stakeholders*, people who are involved with the organization—the people it serves, the community in general, funders, staff, and volunteers. All are joined by a common interest and stake in the organization's outcomes.

Second, the organization uses resources *that have been purchased by the funds of others*. While it's true that the organization earns these funds from others, it is also accountable to them to deliver the outcomes promised in the mission. What a tough position! The leaders in a not-for-profit organization are accountable for something they don't own, so they often have to behave as if they *do* own it. It's easy to slip into the "my" or "our" organization mind-set, if only to rationalize all the hard work and personal sacrifice—but that's the wrong mind-set nevertheless. The stewardship characteristic of humility is perhaps the hardest one to achieve and live by. But until the executive, managers, staff, volunteers, and board "get" the idea that they are truly the stewards of a community resource, they'll be limited in their delivery on the mission.

When you accept the idea that the resources you manage are those of others, what does that look like? What changes will you see? The most important change is that once you truly accept this idea, you'll be more careful.

FOR EXAMPLE: On a Monday you drive your car to the grocery store. You know the route well so you cruise along, anticipating stop signs, turns, and traffic signals. When you get home, your car develops alternator problems and has to go into the repair shop. The next day, you have to go back to the store for something you forgot. Your neighbor is kind enough to lend you her car. Do you drive as casually on Tuesday as you did on Monday? Of course not. It's not your car. You are much, much more careful.

That's how it is once you realize that the management you are doing is for others and with others' resources. It sharpens your management attention—you are "driving someone else's car." So "It's not our stuff" can become a mantra, and keeping that mantra foremost is the first tenet of stewardship and a key driver of decision making. The next is being sure you use the resources to maximum effect.

Corollary: Get maximum return on investment

As a steward, your job is to get the most mission out the door for the benefit of others. You need to use all your resources. Your organization's success in stewardship is manifest in the returns you get on its investments, whether those investments are financial, staff time, or mission activities.

Most of us are familiar with getting a good return on our financial investments. For the steward, all expenditures are *investments in mission*. This is a good thing: it helps you see money spent (or staff time, or whatever the expenditure) not as a loss but as an opportunity. Investments in mission provide opportunities for the people you serve.

But what return on investment should you seek? As an individual, if you are choosing among investment options, you certainly pay attention to the interest or dividend that is paid to you. Higher returns are usually associated with higher risk. So you try to find the best mix of risk and return on your investment. If you are a prudent investor, you research your options thoroughly. As a mission-based steward, you have to be concerned with two returns on investment—the financial return *and* the

> For the steward, all expenditures are *investments in mission* that provide opportunities for the people you serve.

social return (the balance of mission and money). As with strict financial investments, the higher mission/money returns usually are accompanied by higher risk.

When making decisions, the concept of dual return on investment helps you consider things that accomplish lots of mission but don't make money, as well as things that don't accomplish much mission and *must* make money.

> **FOR EXAMPLE**: For an organization with a mission of feeding the hungry, a free soup kitchen is a mission-rich investment, but it does not make any money. That's perfectly fine if funding is in place to run the kitchen. Fundraising, in contrast, usually does nothing directly for the mission. Therefore *it must make money*. So it's often not good stewardship to have the fundraising staff investing lots of time into events that don't result in donations far in excess of expenses, such as special events that wind up generating little profit, or worse, cost the organizations money.

As you begin to wrestle with this concept and its applications, you will see that you can't make good financial or mission stewardship decisions without good information. And, as a result of the way many not-for-profits are funded and are required to do their accounting, there is a lot of bad information out there masquerading as accurate data—much of it the result of cost shifting (a topic we'll deal with later in this book).

Figuring return on investment—whether it is financial investment or mission investment—takes good information. And it is one of those big-think concepts that can shape the way you plan, manage, delegate, and budget. Work to get comfortable with it. The decision-making tool in this chapter will help you see how to act on the concept.

Useful Decision-Making Tools

Whether the issue is mission or money, staff or board, you are going to be making decisions. As a steward, should you seek a particular sequence to that decision process? Yes. On the following page is a stewardship decision model for you to consider. It's adaptable to many situations. We'll look at various uses as we walk through it.

The tool is made up of five decision points, each comprised of one question with several specific components. To move on from one decision point to the next, you *must* have a "Yes" answer *to at least one* component. The more "Yes" answers you get, the better, which you will see as we go through the uses of the model.

As we go through the model, you may well think of component questions you want to add to one or more decision points. That's great. The model allows for, even encourages, customization. Just remember to work through all five key decision points.

The graphic on page 30 will help you visualize the decision process.

You can see that the model is sequential, with the numbered decision points in priority order, and the lettered components all of equal importance. As noted earlier, to proceed from one decision point to the next, you must get at least one "Yes" from a component question. The more yes answers the better. If you get no yes answers, *except in absolutely extraordinary* circumstances, the decision should be to delay or defer.

Why is it important to count yes votes if you get more than one? Because you may well use this tool to weigh various options.

> **FOR EXAMPLE:** In the coming fiscal year you have two options for service expansion. You can expand one kind of service into a new geographical area (a new city, county, state, or country), or you can stay where you are and expand the volume of a different kind of service in the existing locations. Both require an investment of $40,000. How do you decide? One way is to use the tool above. In this case, counting the "yes" votes contained in decision points one and two and comparing them may well help you decide which option is more advantageous, while weighing the yes votes in decision point three will help you decide whether your information on one option is better than the other.

Brinckerhoff's Stewardship Decision Tree

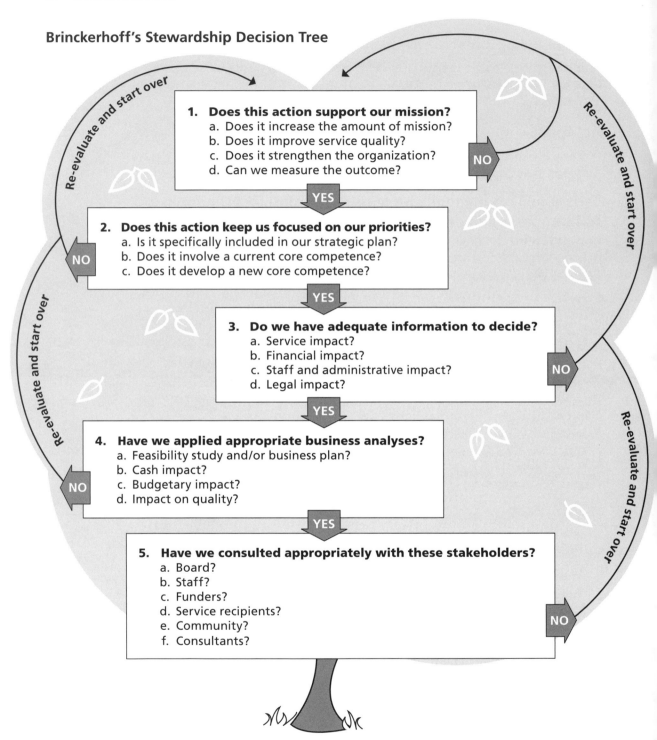

Re-evaluate and start over

1. Does this action support our mission?
a. Does it increase the amount of mission?
b. Does it improve service quality?
c. Does it strengthen the organization?
d. Can we measure the outcome?

NO

YES

2. Does this action keep us focused on our priorities?
a. Is it specifically included in our strategic plan?
b. Does it involve a current core competence?
c. Does it develop a new core competence?

NO

YES

3. Do we have adequate information to decide?
a. Service impact?
b. Financial impact?
c. Staff and administrative impact?
d. Legal impact?

NO

YES

4. Have we applied appropriate business analyses?
a. Feasibility study and/or business plan?
b. Cash impact?
c. Budgetary impact?
d. Impact on quality?

NO

YES

5. Have we consulted appropriately with these stakeholders?
a. Board?
b. Staff?
c. Funders?
d. Service recipients?
e. Community?
f. Consultants?

NO

Re-evaluate and start over

Also understand that a "no" vote on decision points 3, 4, or 5 may well not force a permanent negative decision, but will often simply defer the decision until adequate information, analysis, or consultation has been accomplished.

Let's look at each decision point in a little more depth.

1. Does this action support our mission?

There should be no surprise that mission comes first. But the importance here is the focus on measurable outcome. Look at the component questions: How much more mission work will we do? How much better will we serve the mission? Does it strengthen the organization? Can we measure the outcome?

Remember that as a steward, one of your key focus areas is on the return you get—both in mission outcome and financial benefit. Would you invest in a mutual fund that didn't give you positive outcomes? Of course not. So you need to measure. Further, you need to be concerned about the quality of each "unit of mission" you produce. Finally, a decision that strengthens the organization in the short term or long term may be considered positive.

FOR EXAMPLE: An action to increase the organization's endowment brings no immediate improvement in mission volume or quality, but

---

Brinckerhoff's Stewardship Decision Tree

The Brinckerhoff Stewardship Decision Tree is meant to be *used*. You can copy it from this book or download a free version from Fieldstone Alliance's web site. The downloadable version can be modified so you can document your thinking process. To obtain it, visit this URL and use the following access code:

http://www.FieldstoneAlliance.org/worksheets

Access code: W423Stw04

It's also available at Peter's web site at the following URL:

http://www.missionbased.com/stewardship.htm

it does strengthen the organization, and it is measurable. An action to expand the number of concerts a youth symphony provides is both measurable and increases the mission volume. An action to seek accreditation for the organization results in higher quality in the long run, but probably not in any more mission being immediately provided.

2. Does this action keep us focused on our priorities?

Focus, focus, focus. Good stewards are concerned with what their community needs *and* wants and whether or not the organization can provide for those needs and wants *well*. Just because you *can* do something doesn't mean you *should* do it. This decision point tries to keep you focused on what's important. Look at the component questions: Does the action relate to a strategic plan priority? Does it use an existing core competence or develop a new one?

Clearly implied here is that your organization has a current strategic plan. If it doesn't, you need one—and soon. It is extremely difficult to stay organizationally focused on your priorities if you haven't established those priorities. You need a current plan (see Chapter 6, Planning Your Path).

> **FOR EXAMPLE**: You may have to make a decision about whether to accept funding for a new service population. This funding would increase revenue, but is the new population one you want to pursue? If you already have included that population in your strategic plan, you will have looked at its long-term needs, the state of the art in serving that population, and other factors. If the decision deadline is tight, you can make a better stewardship decision if you have done the planning and prioritizing earlier.

Use the component questions to stay focused.

3. Do we have adequate information to decide?

Sometimes you already have the information necessary to make a decision. In most cases, however, you'll have to go after the information you need. This decision point attempts to strengthen the decision process by reminding you what information is important: What is the mission impact? What is the financial impact? What is the impact on staff and administration? What is the legal impact? All of these component questions should force you to look deeply into your decision and thus be better stewards of your resources. Note that the questions do not ask, "Do we make or lose money?" Rather, they focus on the impact—the overriding goal of stewardship.

> **FOR EXAMPLE**: Don't forget that while expansion of service is great, you should always look at the staff and administrative impact of a decision. Going to expand your staff by 10 percent? Good, but can the human resources department, the payroll function, the square footage you rent or own handle that kind of increase? Such choices sometimes seep into legal questions: if you are expanding or contracting, where do you cross a legal or regulatory line? Do you fall outside of a mandated staff-per-client ratio, or fail to be financially transparent enough for a certain funder?

Of course, you need accurate information to answer this question. We'll talk about this in depth in Chapter 7, Financial Stewardship, but remember here that if you have bad data, you'll make bad decisions. (As the computer programmers say: "Garbage in, garbage out.")

4. Have we applied appropriate business analyses?

Your organization is a mission-based business, one whose stewards use all the resources available to accomplish the mission. The best stewards use not only traditional resources but also business analyses to increase their organization's mission-effectiveness. In decision making, we have a terrific application of this principle. Before you make an investment in mission, shouldn't you use the best tools to decide? Those tools are referred to in the component questions here: Have you done a feasibility study, developed a business plan, and analyzed cash-flow impacts as well as the impact on your budget?

Since any investment has a certain amount of risk, you want to make that risk reasonable and as small as possible. Business techniques can help you do that. We'll go into the application of business plans and feasibility studies in Chapter 8, Taking Good Risk. Just remember that you can't scoot past these just because the mission outcome is strong, or because the idea looks like a "sure thing."

> **FOR EXAMPLE**: You might have the opportunity to consider some funding for a new program. You look at your budget and see that for overall budget purposes you will come out fine. But then you study the cash-flow impact and discover that you will wind up $40,000 short this fiscal year since the funder pays so slowly after you provide the service. Go ahead or not? Your call, but now you have the information you need and have used two good business tools.

While not all decisions require a feasibility study or a business plan, pretty much every resource allocation does require a review of your budget and the cash-flow implications. (You may want to amend the decision tool to require two "yes" votes from this decision point, and mandate both a budget and cash-flow analysis before proceeding.)

5. Have we consulted appropriately?

You can't make every decision by committee. You can't make every decision by consensus. You can't make every decision alone. Thus, this decision point focuses on appropriate consultation, and the component questions give you a wide range of possible types of people to consult: board, staff, volunteers, funders, service recipients, community, and—indeed—consultants.

Consultation is one of those balance challenges. You want the insights and perspective of others, yet you don't want decisions to be undermined by endless discussion. As Max DePree says in his wonderful book *Leading Without Power*, not-for-profits far too often "seek acceptance rather than agreement."[3] DePree means that reliance on consensus subjects the organization to a jury model of decision making in which everyone

---

[3] Max DePree, *Leading Without Power: Finding Hope in Serving Community* (San Francisco: Jossey-Bass, 1997), 57.

Using Outsiders to Inform Decisions

A successful not-for-profit organization will use a variety of people resources as it pursues its mission, including staff, board members, and nongoverning volunteers, all of whom are *insiders* with regard to the organization. But people who are *outside* the organization have a perspective that can be vital to good decision making. They are also less prone to inherent conflicts of interest than insiders.

For example, if you have to lay off some staff you have a conflict of interest. Presumably you know these people and their families, and you may be tempted to take extraordinary, and sometimes organizationally unwise, measures to keep them employed. Similarly a board member who has a relative served by the organization may not bring complete objectivity to discussions about the services received by that family member. Neither of these situations is unusual, nor are they inherently bad. But an outsider can help provide a less emotional, more detached analysis.

Here are several ways to use outsiders:

- Convene groups of stakeholders to collect information and perspectives that can help you make decisions.

- Add non-board members to certain board committees to help with decisions. For example, find people who are interested in a particular issue, such as finance or fundraising, and have them give their time and energy, but spare them the responsibility and larger commitment of being on the board. (Added benefit: some of these people may go on to become board members as they build their personal investment in the organization's mission.)

- Use "targeted volunteers"—people with special connections or expertise required for only a limited time. For example, you need a survey of service recipients, but you don't know how to do it. You find a local recruit to work just on this project for a limited time. **Note:** Never use this technique if the work product might result in a liability—for example, don't recruit a volunteer for legal work, accounting, architectural drawings, or a review of your personnel policies. For those kinds of needs, be prepared to pay.

- Hire consultants to provide technical assistance—to fill a short-term need such as conducting focus groups, conducting an audit, or doing a site analysis, or to provide organization development assistance such as facilitating planning processes, decisions, and change.

Outsiders can provide expertise and perspective. In some cases they are paid, in others they are volunteers. Always be looking to bring resources from both inside and outside the organization to bear on your problems and challenges.

must be convinced before the organization can do anything. That's a 500-pound weight around the neck of any manager. Stewards must make decisions and be held responsible for the results of those decisions. One of the benefits of working in a not-for-profit environment is that you can call on lots of people to help you in your decision making, depending on the situation. So when should the wise steward consult with others?

- Decisions on borrowing, new programs, purchases, budgeting, or policies should involve the board of directors and committee structure. The idea of a board is to provide outside, objective checks and balances on your staff work.

- Involve staff at every level in decision making to get feedback on what works and what doesn't. Ask, consult, and put staff from all levels of the organization on your internal committees.

- Consult your community and your service recipients about marketing activities. Only by asking these people what they want can you provide services in a manner that will ensure wide use and mission outcomes. Whether through surveys, focus groups, or informal information gathering, asking questions is a very real engine for organizational improvement and efficient and effective mission provision.

- Use outside consultation for decisions on annual audit, legal advice, or keeping your personnel policies current.

So now you have a decision-making tool that you can apply in a variety of situations. You'll be seeing it again and again in the coming chapters.

Recap

In this chapter we've examined the key idea about stewardship—*It's not your organization*—and how that plays out in decisions. We looked at the issue of return on investment and ways to evaluate both the mission return and the financial return. Finally, we put everything together with a multipurpose decision-making tool for you to use. You'll see variations on it later in the book.

By now you should have a good handle on theory and applications when it comes to stewardship. But the *implementation* of stewardship varies with a person's role in the organization. The next three chapters will deal, in order, with the various interlocking stewardship roles of board members, staff, and funders.

CHAPTER TWO DISCUSSION QUESTIONS

1. Are we focused enough on mission? How can we do more in this area? What ideas can we act on today?

2. Do we think of expenses as investments? How do we measure mission outcome now? Financial outcome?

3. Should we have outsiders on board committees? Why or why not? What about consultants? Do we use them appropriately?

4. What do we think of the decision model? Do we have questions to add to each decision point's components? Is this flexible enough for us to use in a variety of situations? What are some typical situations where we could have used the tool in the past—and how might we apply it in the future?

PART II

Implementing
Stewardship

CHAPTER THREE # Board Stewardship

N ow that you have the basic concepts of stewardship under your belt and have looked at some particular applications of the model, it's time to apply the model to specific roles in your organization.

We'll start with your board of directors. Why? Because board members—when performing the roles that they should, in the ways that they should, with the skill set that they need—best personify stewardship. Board members are personally responsible for the uses of your organization's resources, and yet the vast majority of board members never benefit personally from their board work. They spend their time, their talent, and, in many cases, their personal funds to support the organization *for the benefit of others*.

Boards should work in partnership with their employees, their community, their funders, and all the other varied stakeholders who are affected by the organization's mission. Like all stewards, they need to balance needs and wants, money and mission.

Sounds pretty good, doesn't it? The problem is, governance issues rank just behind money shortages in the struggles that not-for-profit organizations face. "My board president wants to control everything I do" is one common refrain. So are "My board president won't let other board members talk," and "Our staff don't get us board members the information we need."

At many large conferences, workshops on "Working with Your Board," "Appropriate Decision Tools for Board Members," "Evaluating the Board of Directors," and "Improving Board-Staff Relations" are always well attended, sometimes with standing room only.

While the theory behind not-for-profit governance is great, implementation is an issue that vexes thousands of boards and staff. The information, ideas, and perspective in this chapter may help solve these problems for your organization. How? Because one of the starting points in getting more from yourself and your board is taking on the stewardship mindset: "It's someone else's stuff, not *ours*." As many board consultants will tell you, problem solving with boards often comes down to turf battles or control issues. Giving up on the idea that the organization is yours to control, yours to fight over, can be a real achievement and a significant move forward. This chapter will discuss that, as well as many practical ways to improve board performance and stewardship.

We'll start by looking at the board's role as a group. Taking a stewardship mind-set, we'll walk through the key responsibilities of policy setting, checks and balances, and liability, and then examine a list of board responsibilities. Next, we'll look at two key people on the board—the president and the treasurer—and how they can best help steward the organization. We'll examine their unique roles and detail the things they can do to help—or hinder—the organization's quest for mission enhancement.

Finally, we'll turn to the very important issue of board liability and how to reduce it. You want great board members who can be wonderful stewards, but you can't attract or retain such people if they are worried about their own personal risk any more than is absolutely necessary.

And remember this: board members, like all stewards, are *temporary* stewards. None of us will be here forever. So how can we make this year, this month, this *meeting* the most valuable to our mission outcome? Keep that in mind as you read this chapter, and by its end, you'll have a great set of tools to improve the stewardship capabilities of your board.

The Board's Stewardship Role

The board of directors should be working for the benefit of the community, first, last, and in between. As stewards, the board members' job is to manage community resources as efficiently and effectively as possible, enabling the organization to deliver the highest-quality mission it can—back to the community. The bottom line is not organizational survival, or budget growth, or hiring more staff. It's service to the community, using the resources the community has entrusted the board with.

With that as our foundation, let's look at some practical issues. In any well-run not-for-profit, a balance is struck between the board and staff. In fact, the role of each in relation to the other is just that—a check and a balance. If the organization gets out of balance, it doesn't function well. Like any other balancing act, this takes practice and consistent work. In terms of organizational policy there is a need for balance as well, one that we have discussed at length: the balance between mission and money.

There is no question that the final decision on any major policy decision is the responsibility of the board. Boards, after all, set policy. If the board feels that the organization's assets are theirs (either literally, or on behalf of the organization), a stewardship mind-set is hard to attain and harder to retain. For people who have put in years on the board, who may even be founders, who may have donated huge amounts of time, talent, and treasure to the mission, it is understandably difficult to stand back and say, "Okay, it's not ours, it's the community's." This certainly gets in the way of taking risks, or trying new things, or even recognizing weaknesses in the organization's capabilities to provide services. As board members, we can often get so full of ourselves, we forget that the point is mission to others. After all, we're only human.

> FOR EXAMPLE: Dave, a long-serving elder of a huge congregation, was intimately involved in the decision to triple the size of the church on a new site. He attended hundreds of planning meetings and went to the construction site every day for three years to document progress and make sure that the construction crew was doing the right things. No one put in more hours than Dave.

For board stewards, the bottom line is not organizational survival, or budget growth, or hiring more staff. It's *service to the community,* using the resources the community has entrusted the board with.

About a year after the church building was dedicated, I asked Dave how things were shaking out with the building, and how the debt had affected the church finances. He said that the building was working out very well, and that the finances were better than anyone had anticipated. Interest rates had dropped, the finance committee had refinanced the mortgage, and so far, so good. Or, as Dave said: "God has been very good to us. He's given us a great facility in which to do His work." I asked whether he would agree that some people (like Dave himself) had just a bit to do with it as well. Dave smiled, and then said, "Y'know, there are some people on the board who spent some time recently congratulating all of us and, frankly, it was nice to get the kudos. I was pleased to hear all these good people, my friends, speak out about what a great job I had done. Then our minister brought us back into focus on our mission by reading Psalm 24, verses 1 & 2. We were humbled, and got back on track."

Focus (and Celebrate) Your Mission

One way to constantly bring your focus back to the right place is to regularly celebrate the outcomes of your mission. No doubt your organization has legions of stories about "Johnny" who was at point "X" when he first visited and now is at point "ten times X" because of what your organization does. A great way for boards to focus on and celebrate the mission is to have a brief (maximum two minutes) "Johnny story" early in every meeting. Make sure the storyteller relates the story back to the mission of the organization. These stories humble, focus, and renew boards over and over again.

This works for many different organizations, not just those who work in human services. A performing arts group regularly read letters from elementary students (or their parents) telling how moved they were at a particular concert. An animal rescue shelter group started every meeting with before-and-after pictures of an animal saved by the shelter in the previous month. An immigrant literacy group played short audiotapes of thanks from immigrants who had learned English— tapes that showed off their new skills. Be creative with this. But don't let it take more than two minutes per meeting.

Not being a biblical scholar, I went home and looked up the passage. Here's the passage: *"The earth is the Lord's, and all it contains, the world, and those who dwell on it."*

Dave's pastor had reminded them that they were stewards of the gifts they had been given. All of us need to be reminded about the point every once in a while.

Keys to Stewardship

A key to ensuring good board stewardship is achieving the difficult balance between mission and money. To help find and maintain that balance, try to attract and retain two fundamentally different perspectives on your board: those of advocates and businesspeople. We touched on this when we looked at the importance of a businesslike board (page 18). Advocates passionately believe in the mission or the organization and keep it focused on mission, mission, mission. Businesspeople understand and are passionate about finance, marketing, human resources, and other business issues and keep the organization focused on that second rule of not-for-profits: "No money, no mission!"

Having both kinds of people on your board provides a wonderful dynamic tension that helps keep the organization in balance. You may well find both perspectives in one person now and then but make sure you do have a significant number of both groups on your board.

That said, stewardship success isn't just about attaining the right mix of advocates and businesspeople. Boards have key functions to perform.[4] Let's look at the most important stewardship factors in each of the following:

1. Setting and updating policy
2. Serving as a check-and-balance
3. Providing outside credibility

---

[4] Many books provide detailed lists of board functions, including my book *Mission-Based Management*. The list in this book is generalized to show the overarching need for stewardship in board decision making. Adapt it as needed, thinking through the stewardship model's relationship to functions that are critical to your organization.

1. Setting and updating policy

The boards of directors' first job is to set the course for the organization. This is called, in the jargon of organization management, "policy." Policy bears on such things as deciding to add a new service or suspend an existing service, taking on a debt, purchasing or leasing new program space, adopting a budget, developing a strategic plan, setting priorities on services, community needs, and service recipients, and a host of other important long-range decisions.

On the other hand, many boards get distracted from looking at the big picture. To be specific: policy is *not* deciding what color the invitations should be for the annual meeting. It is *not* deciding whether to purchase your office supplies from Staples or OfficeMax. It is *not* spending an hour at every board meeting rehashing what a committee has already spent two hours working through. No doubt you recognize these examples, or could add some from your own board. We all do this at times. But we need to avoid these distractions, because true policy is big-picture stuff. And policy is a crucial stewardship job, since only the board, composed (ideally) of objective semi-outsiders, can (in league with paid professional staff) set the best course to get the most mission out of available resources. If board members are mired in minutiae, or are trying to do the staff's job, it's not a good use of board time. Good board stewards focus on big-picture policy, not minutiae.

2. Serving as a check and balance

Board members, as community representatives, should keep a unique perspective on the organization's priorities and competencies, thereby acting as a check and balance against staff desires to move in too many directions.

> FOR EXAMPLE: Your organization provides services to young children from economically disadvantaged families. You started ten years ago, at first just providing meals and after-school activities. That grew into twelve-month day care, youth development, mentoring, and other needed programs. Your organization is well respected in the low-income neighborhoods where you operate. About

six months ago, the local senior services not-for-profit went bank-rupt and pulled its services out of your neighborhoods. Now the state Department on Aging is coming to your staff suggesting that, since you have such a great reputation in the community and since you already do day care, why don't you start providing day care for seniors as well?

What to do? Often the staff is very excited about a new program, a new funding stream, a new way to help. And in those cases, it is usually the board that asks the tough, necessary questions such as "What in the world do we know about providing services to senior citizens?" or "We're a *youth* organization. I know there is a need for this and money in this, but should we spread ourselves that thin?"

Many executive directors *hate* questions like these from board members. The questions are a terrible hassle and seem to get in the way of doing good things. Of course, often the board is right. Because it is a little removed, it has some perspective and helps keep the organization in balance.

Boards keep things in balance by being well educated about the issues (also a staff responsibility) and being well informed about the organiza-tion (another staff responsibility). But they must also be prepared for meetings (a board responsibility) and must ask lots of questions (another board responsibility—enabled by the board president).

Stewardship mandates that boards work in a consistent manner to maxi-mize mission, balancing the needs of the community with the resources available. Tough job.

3. Providing outside credibility

This job may sound minor in relation to the other two; it is not. Be-cause there is so much cynicism about not-for-profit fundraising, service provision, administrative spending, and quality, your organization needs knowledgeable governing volunteers who are willing to stand up and say credible, good things about the organization.

To provide credibility, board members can accompany staff at interviews for corporate or foundation funding, present to the local chamber of commerce or civic organizations, attend open houses or press briefings on new services, and be present at times of crisis.

Another way that boards provide credibility is through their names. People are more likely to donate or volunteer when they see the names of friends and neighbors they know and trust on a board. A credible, balanced board can make the difference between getting or not getting funding for a certain request, or the difference between recruiting or not recruiting a valuable new board or staff member.

Wise Use of the Board

Using the board wisely is key to good stewardship. Following are some ideas to make your board and its deliberations more effective.

Focus on mission

Keep your mission in front of the board at all times. First, have the board president or committee chair read the mission statement aloud at the start of each board or committee meeting. Then keep lots of copies of it on the table at every meeting of the board and its committees. Board members can refer to the mission statement in mid-discussion and then say, "It seems that we're down to two choices here, and I think choice A is more supportive of the mission as I read it." This will help keep the board (and the organization) focused on what's important.

Check your bylaws

Check your organization's bylaws. They are really the underlying operating rules for your board. Make sure that they do at least the following:

- List the procedure for electing board members
- List terms of office for board members
- List the duties of the board members
- List the titles, duties, terms and method of election of board officers
- Include means to remove a board member and/or an officer
- Discuss policies you don't enforce
- Include conflict-of-interest policies
- Meet local, state, and federal requirements, as well as any mandates added to that list by key funders

Many books offer much more detailed lists of board tasks; some of these can be found in the resource section at the end of this book. However, these three general responsibilities encompass nearly all of the more detailed task lists. They are the best place to start as you consider ways to bring your board into a more steward-based mind-set.

Enough on boards in general. Let's look how the board president can practice stewardship.

Orient the board

Make board orientation ongoing. Boards can't retain everything in one sitting. Make board orientation a fifteen-minute part of every board meeting, working your way through programs, key funding streams, program jargon, conflict-of-interest policies, committee structure, and so forth. Call these sessions "board updates," and put them just before you discuss your financials to ensure the best attendance and most active listening and participation. Remember, stewards value lifelong learning, and the board needs to model that value.

Recruit wisely

Recruitment and turnover are costly, so recruit carefully and select the best board members. Once you get the ideal board member, good stewardship warrants keeping pre-term turnover to a minimum. To avoid loss of new recruits, start a board mentoring program. Assign a senior board member as the new member's mentor. The mentor's job is to meet the new member before the first meeting, introduce them at that initial session, sit next to them for the next six meetings (to answer all the new member's questions), and check in with the new member after the first few meetings to make sure that they understand what's going on and to get them quickly on the inside track.

The Role of the Board President as Steward

The board president (or board chair) truly has a key role. He or she sets the tone in terms of behavior. Serious or silly? Ethical or shady? Watch the president. He or she runs the meetings, efficiently or poorly. Does one person dominate or does everyone get to be heard? The president decides. He or she speaks for the organization, knowledgeably or off the cuff. The board president is the leader of the volunteers, and to many in the community, the most visible person in the organization.

Just as the executive director leads the staff by deed more than word, so it is for the board president. Many decisions, particularly about policy, can only start with the board president, and can certainly end there. A new idea, a major policy change, a suggestion for expansion or collaboration probably have to pass the "board president test" to proceed to the board.

One such innovation is the concept of stewardship. If the president "gets" the stewardship idea, then it is much more likely to happen than if he or she has to be convinced of its value.

The board president has specific impact on stewardship through three key overarching roles:

1. Managing the board of directors
2. Working with the executive director
3. Connecting with the community

1. Managing the board of directors

Managing the board is the most visible part of the board president's job. This includes setting the board agenda and running the meetings with a mix of discipline, advocacy, and order. The board president will probably also help decide who is on which committee, and should help in recruiting new board members.

But it is in the board meeting that the president does the hardest work. It is the president's responsibility to see that the meeting starts and ends on

---

The board president is key to making stewardship a reality. If your board president is not reading this book, consider sharing it with him or her.

time, follows the agenda, and, most importantly, that everyone who wants to speak on a particular issue is heard, without any one person dominating the discussion.

> **FOR EXAMPLE:** When I began my tenure as board president of our local Association of Retarded Citizens, I instituted a number of changes, the most painful of which was starting on time, since starting late punishes those people who arrive on time. At my first meeting, I announced this and other changes, such as a revised agenda, a scheduled ending time for meetings, and a time allocation for each agenda item. I warned everyone that we *would* start at seven o'clock sharp and that we *would* end by nine o'clock. Of course, the next month, only about half the board was there at seven. And we started. By seven-fifteen the rest of the members had straggled in. The last one in the door interrupted the discussion, then asked for a recap of what we had covered already. I refused, telling him that I would be happy to fill him in after the meeting. He was not happy, but he was never late for a meeting again.

It's hard to achieve the balance between encouraging fair, open discussions and keeping the agenda moving so that the board can carefully consider all of the items. Often, a particular agenda item seems to be a life-or-death issue to one person or another. Moving them along is hard.

The **stewardship role** for the president in board and meeting management is to manage the meetings for good use of resources and time, and to regularly remind the board that they are managing the resources of others. This is a never-ending series of reminders, coaching, and observations. The president should set the tone with her or his actions and words and then gently bring the rest of the board along.

2. Working with the executive director

The second role for the board president is working with the executive director in a manner that embodies the policy and check-and-balance functions of the board, with the added tasks of supporting, coaching, and serving as a sounding board.

The board president is the board member who spends the most time with the executive director, either on the phone, via e-mail, or in person. Thus, the president stands in for the board in many situations, and as a result is the first arbiter or filter in terms of the policies that the board will consider. He or she should always be thinking about the large picture when dealing with the executive, and should attempt to bring an objective viewpoint to the discussion.

A crucial role for the board president is that of a sounding board (and a safe place to vent) for the executive director. Not-for-profit executives have a very lonely job. There is rarely, if ever, anyone they can confide in who truly understands their problems and concerns. Without CEO expe-

HANDS-ON

Stewardship Tips for the Board President

Use meeting time wisely

Don't let discussions stall or loop back to the same points. To move a discussion along, ask "Okay, does anyone have anything *new* to add to the discussion?" Don't ask, "Does anyone have anything *else* to say?" This usually results in a few people saying the same thing they said four minutes earlier.

Keep committee topics in committee, not in full board meetings. Finance, fundraising, and other committees should meet between board meetings, discuss their special issues, and make recommendations to the board. This spreads the work, can bring nonboard experts into the discussion, and allows adequate time to cover critical issues without taking up the time of the entire board. Don't use board time to repeat committee meetings. If board members begin to review committee minutiae during a full board meeting, stop them, either privately or publicly. Tell them that you appreciate their concern for the issue, and that they are welcome to go to the relevant committee meetings, but that full board meeting discussions (absent a huge crisis) need to be short and to the point. Don't tell them that they shouldn't care, just channel their inquiries to the proper forum.

Set time limits on the agenda. Give your agenda a start time, an end time, and a time limit for each item. This lets people know there are limits and, assuming the entire board sets those limits, establishes priorities. The board president should enforce the limits.

rience, even the board president can't really understand. But they can and should listen, and they can provide a place where the executive can come to test an idea without taking it to the whole board right away.

Thus the president needs to be able to listen, to respond, and to not repeat everything he or she hears to the rest of the board after every conversation with the executive.

The board president's second **stewardship role** is to manage the crucial resource of the top staff person, keeping him or her on track, as happy as possible, and certainly feeling supported.

Support your executive

Build trust with your executive. Board presidents should schedule regular one-on-one lunch or breakfast updates with the organization's executive, at least once between every board meeting. Review key items such as the upcoming board agenda, major issues that the board will cover, and so forth. But also ask the executive how he or she is doing and then just listen. Do this consistently to build the rapport and trust that will strengthen the organization. This does not mean that the executive and board president can (or even should) be best friends. But a good working relationship benefits all.

Take care with the community

Get some training on dealing with stakeholders. By virtue of role, the board president is a key liaison to the community—internal and external. It takes practice to learn how to identify stakeholder groups and convene, listen to, and learn from them. Handling one stakeholder group—the media—requires special training. Therefore, avoid the trap of *automatically* making the board president the organization's media spokesperson, since the board president may not be the best spokesperson. Establish media policies that designate a spokesperson to deal with the press *in any and all situations, good or bad.* Whether that person is the board president or someone else, get them trained to interact with the media.

3. Connecting with the community

The board president is the "ceremonial" community liaison on behalf of the volunteers of the organization. While you may well have a staff person whose job is to maximize the positive image of the organization in the community, the president is often asked to speak or be present at a Rotary meeting or United Way dinner simply because of the title "board president." So select a president with these skills and recruit officers who are comfortable in public, who can do a short public speech reasonably well, and who are willing to put in the time to be knowledgeable about the organization's services and challenges.

The second community role for the board president is internal. Staff and volunteers are motivated when the board president (if not other board members) attends a staff recognition lunch, or a celebration of organizational accreditation, or other award ceremonies. It is also important for a president to be there if a staff person dies or if a severe personal crisis occurs among the staff. Ceremony *does* matter, and good presidents know that and act on it.

The board president's **stewardship role** is to show the community and the staff that the board is managing its resources well, wisely, and in support of its charitable mission.

That's a big load for anyone. So get your president some help—he or she is far too important a resource to waste. If your management support organization or your local college not-for-profit program has training in running meetings, or even in being a board president, get your president to attend. Check out online courses for them, and look for books and workbooks that may help them do their job better. Some are listed in the Resource section on page 233.

Now let's look at another crucial officer—your board treasurer.

The Role of the Board Treasurer

Clearly, financial stewardship is a crucial part of overall resource management. In fact, when you say the word "steward," most people first think of money. (Well, some people would answer "wine" but that's a topic for another book.) In your not-for-profit, the money stuff is handled on the board by the board treasurer and (ideally) the finance committee, which the treasurer should chair.

A board treasurer has a truly important and truly thankless task. He or she has three overarching things to accomplish:

1. Understand the organization's financials

2. Measure financial return on investment

3. Report credibly

1. Understand the financials

At least one person on the board needs to deeply understand the organization's finances. For most not-for-profits, that's the treasurer. First, having someone who truly "gets it" is crucial to the check-and-balance function. A board without a financial expert cannot truly make good stewardship decisions related to finance. Second, having such a board person allows the rest of the board to relax a bit and not obsess on managing the money. Instead of worrying about the accuracy of the financials or their implications at every board meeting, the board can do what it should be doing—maximizing the mission.

2. Measure financial return on investment

The treasurer, along with the chief financial employee, is the person who is really responsible for measuring the financial return on investment that the organization is getting from any decision. The board has to be able to turn to a peer and say, "What's the financial outcome of this action, and how good or how bad is it?" That peer is the treasurer. (Details on measuring return on investment are covered in Chapter 7, Financial Stewardship.)

3. Report credibly

It's one thing to understand an issue. It's another to be able to explain it so that others understand it and feel comfortable with it. A treasurer needs to do both. Board members, though personally responsible for the actions of the organization, come with a wide range of financial experience and expertise. It doesn't make sense to send every board member to accounting school, nor would it benefit the organization for the board to consist solely of accountants. Board members should try to understand everything they can about the organization, including its finances, and staff members should do everything they can to facilitate that learning. But there regularly comes a point when board members need credible, understandable information to make a decision. And it's easier (and better management practice) for the board to make a decision if they know that a knowledgeable treasurer agrees.

Thus the treasurer serves as a check and balance, a technician, and a messenger to the rest of the board, as well as an occasional spokesperson to community organizations and funders. That's a load. There is an old, old saying: "If Momma ain't happy, nobody's happy." Turn that around for your treasurer. If your treasurer is happy—has the support and the tools to do the job—then the treasurer can stop perseverating over every dime and relax a bit. A relaxed treasurer is more likely to be able to sit back and make good, objective stewardship decisions about the funds that are in your organization's keeping. So get them the help they need.

In Chapter 7, we'll discuss other ways to help your treasurer, as well as the rest of your board and staff, by providing reports that facilitate easier decisions.

Reducing Board Liability Is Good Stewardship

Remember, your board is a key resource, one to be used to the fullest benefit of your mission. A resource is less than well used if it is put at unreasonable risk. Just as you install sprinklers or smoke alarms to reduce risk, you should take steps to protect the board.

Should You Have a Vice-Treasurer?

Pity your poor treasurer. First the treasurer must journey into the organizational labyrinth of finance, understand it deeply, and come back to explain the financial mysteries to the rest of the board. Once the treasurer achieves this success, he or she is often stuck in the job. A good treasurer is so valuable no one wants them to go. To solve this problem, do for your treasurer what you probably already do with your board president: establish an ascendancy protocol. Find someone to be assistant treasurer or vice-treasurer. Put this role in your bylaws. This person can chair the finance committee in the absence of the treasurer, and slowly learn to replace the treasurer at some point down the road. Besides, what could be wrong with *two* people on your board really "getting" your financials?

Who Staffs the Finance Committee?

The treasurer should chair your finance committee. For staff, choose the person who has the most interaction with and the deepest understanding of the organization's finances. In a very small organization, that might be the executive director, but for most, it will be the director of finance or chief financial officer (CFO). The board treasurer needs more staff time than any other volunteer with the possible exception of the president. So let the relationship between the treasurer and CFO develop and work for you.

Besides the treasurer and CFO, consider expanding the committee to include a few financial experts who are *not* on the board. Get some dispassionate outside experts—perhaps someone from the chamber of commerce, a finance professor from the local college or university, or a CFO from a local company. There are lots of people in your community who would be happy to help but don't want to be on the board.

Finally, consider having a smaller finance team to work on such things as debt strategy, financial ratios, and financial goal setting. This work group should be comprised of your CFO, your treasurer, your assistant treasurer, your banker, and your auditor. Get them together once or twice a year to review your financials and to look ahead a bit. They might discuss projections on interest rates, look at new accounting reporting requirements, and address other finance issues.

First some background, then some "how-to." Board members are *fiduciaries*. That is, they are *personally* responsible for the outcomes of the organization and the responsible use of its funds. This personal responsibility is very real, and is the reason that you no longer see not-for-profit letterhead of the type you did twenty years ago—the type that listed numerous politicians, all of whom served on multiple boards. They didn't go to all those meetings but they allowed their name to be used for clout. No longer. Why? Because of their personal liability.

Worse than just being liable for personal error, if you are a board member, you are *liable for things done in your absence*. You are responsible for staff errors. You are also responsible for the actions of the board taken at any meeting, *even ones that you did not attend*. That's why the politician's names no longer grace dozens of not-for-profits' letterheads. They couldn't possibly be at all those meetings.

Board members also present a risk to the organization through their own actions. If board members flaunt their position for personal or familial gain, or if they abuse their authority by pursuing a vendetta against staff members, they risk, and perhaps permanently sacrifice, the reputation, the funding, or the functionality of the organization that they are charged with stewarding. This is why you need good board training, good board role models, and, most importantly, a working conflict-of-interest policy.

A *conflict-of-interest policy* is a document that states what is and what is not acceptable in terms of board members (and staff members) benefiting from their association with the organization. The policy should define what a conflict is and how to work through it. It may well state that no board members may contract with the organization for anything. Neither can members of their families—or their firms, for professionals such as lawyers, accountants, and physicians. Easily done in large cities. A whole lot tougher in small towns, which may have a limited supply of lawyers, accountants, or licensed plumbers (all of which will be needed by the organization at some point).

How stringent your conflict-of-interest policy is depends on three factors: funder requirements, community, and recent scandals. Some funders, notably from the federal government, adamantly favor a very exclusive conflict-of-interest policy, one where board members and their families cannot contract in any way at any time for any reason with the organization. However, as noted, smaller towns usually have fewer vendors available, and therefore often have a less exclusive policy. Finally, recent scandals—that is, someone in town got caught with their finger in the pie—usually result in tighter financial and conflict-of-interest policies.

A conflict-of-interest policy that is both in place and actively enforced is good stewardship; it preserves your hard-earned funds as well as your hard-earned reputation. If you don't have a policy, talk to your state not-for-profit association, your local United Way, or your local management support organization to see what others have done and to see sample

Preventing Conflict of Interest

You have fire drills, right? Training the board on your conflict-of-interest policy is a similar preventive measure. Once a year, have a thirty-minute refresher session at a board meeting. Don't just read through it. Talk through the policy, giving examples of what it *means*: "Fred, this means that if your wife's firm wanted to bid on our computer upgrade contract, that she would have to..." Be specific. Leave time for questions. Train, train, train.

Once you have the conflict-of-interest policy in place and have trained on it thoroughly, you need to secure commit-

ment. Every board member should sign a form similar to the following:

I, [board member's name], have read the conflict-of-interest policy dated [date of adoption], have had the policy explained to me, have had the opportunity to ask questions about the policy, and I agree to abide by the policy.

Signature _____
Date _____

Keep these on file. They're the best prevention for what an attorney friend calls the "But nobody told me" defense.

HANDS-ON

policies. Go online to look for good examples. Don't reinvent the wheel, but do make sure the policy fits your unique mix of funding, community, and culture.

But just having the policy is not enough. Once you get a policy developed and approved by the board, there are two other things to do—teach the policy and secure signed commitments. The sidebar Preventing Conflict of Interest, page 59, tells how to do this.

With conflict of interest out of the way (or perhaps *on* the way if you don't have a policy now), let's turn to a list of practices to reduce board liability. These include

- Go to meetings and go prepared
- Ask questions: Silence is not innocence
- Read the financials carefully
- Get an outside audit and a management letter each year
- Carry Directors and Officers insurance

Go to meetings and go prepared

If you are not at a meeting, how can you influence what's being decided? Absence does not equal innocence for a fiduciary. Go to the meetings. And go having read your meeting materials thoroughly, listing any questions that may need answering. If the board is voting on a controversial issue and decides in a manner that you disagree with, ask to have your name recorded in dissent in the minutes of the meeting—and then make sure you review those minutes when they are distributed!

Ask questions: Silence is not innocence

Ask your questions. My first board president used to say: "The only dumb question is the one that doesn't get asked." As noted immediately above, read your materials and come prepared with your questions. Ask, ask, ask—but pick your forum wisely. Some questions can easily be answered by a phone call to the appropriate staff person. Don't take up the time of the entire board asking, for example, for a copy of a particular marketing pamphlet. But many other questions should be asked in front of the board. Protect yourself and do your job: ask.

Read the financials carefully

Money management is crucial, and problems with finances are often one of the first indicators of trouble. In Chapter 7, Financial Stewardship, you'll see a reporting format that will make reading and understanding your financials much easier. This is important not only to reduce your liability, but also to make sure that you are fulfilling your stewardship responsibilities. Read the numbers, compare them to your budget, and where there are large discrepancies, ask, ask, ask!

Get an outside audit and a management letter each year

Hire a competent accounting firm, bidding the work out to new vendors every three years, to do a complete audit and send a management letter directly to the board. This will help ensure not only that funds are being spent according to contract provisions, but that all state, federal, local, and funder requirements are fulfilled. The management letter advises the board of any structural or policy changes that may be needed to make the organization more fiscally secure and responsible. Don't scrimp on this service.

Carry Directors and Officers insurance

Directors and Officers ("D & O") insurance protects board members from liability in the normal course of operations. Purchase it *if and only if* the insurance buys you more protection than your state volunteer protection statute offers. (The federal government and nearly all states have such laws.)

Here's the mantra on risk: "Reasonable risk, good. Liability, bad." Your board should regularly, as a part of its stewardship role, be taking good risk on behalf of the people you serve. But they should also work to reduce board (and organizational) liability to the greatest extent possible.

Recap

In this chapter, we looked at how board members can help your organization as it pursues stewardship as a value. First we examined the role of the board as a whole, including its roles, responsibilities, and how its decisions can best enhance the mission of the organization. You learned some hands-on ideas to apply at your next board meeting, ideas about use of mission statements, regular board orientation, and, for the longer term, mentoring practices for new board members.

Remember, boards need two kinds of people: advocates for your mission, and businesspeople to balance out the mission-versus-money struggle every not-for-profit goes through. Once you have both kinds, then you can deal with implementing stewardship principles in the three main areas of board responsibility:

1. Setting and updating policy
2. Serving as a check-and-balance
3. Providing outside credibility

Then we looked at two important roles on the board of directors: the president and the treasurer. Each is crucial to the efficient and effective functioning of the organization. First we examined the special functions of the president:

• Managing the board of directors
• Working with the executive director
• Connecting with the community

The board president can make or break the stewardship model from the board's perspective—just as the executive director can influence staff on staff stewardship (as we will see in the next chapter). We looked at a few ways to train and support the board president.

The treasurer's role is vital. To be good stewards, board members must trust the treasurer, and the treasurer must fully understand the finances of the organization. Without those two key elements, the ability of the board to focus comfortably on nonfinancial issues is reduced dramatically. We also noted the need for an assistant treasurer to help the treasurer and create a succession path.

Finally, we dealt with the issue of board liability and ways to reduce it, including some advice on conflict-of-interest policies. These included attending meetings, coming prepared, asking questions, and obtaining Directors & Officers insurance.

So now you have learned about the first of the three specific roles we'll cover—board stewardship. We have two more to go: staff and funders. In the next chapter, we'll look at staff stewardship in detail.

CHAPTER THREE DISCUSSION QUESTIONS

1. Do we think of our board (or, do we think of ourselves, if the board is using this book) as a valuable resource or as an obstacle to progress? Do we see ourselves as a support and resource to the organization or as "owners" of the organization?

2. Do we have the skills we need on the board? How can we improve our recruitment to fill the skill slots we need?

3. How can we regularly orient our board more effectively? (For example, should we include fifteen minutes of orientation per meeting?)

4. Do we have a good mix of mission advocates and businesspeople on our board?

5. How can we be more supportive and helpful to our board president?

6. Are we staffing our board committees appropriately? Do the staff members assisting the committees have adequate resources and training?

7. Should we consider an assistant treasurer? Who would that be?

CHAPTER FOUR

Staff and Volunteer Stewardship

With our governing volunteers (the board of directors) covered, we need to look at stewardship issues for employees and for the volunteers who serve staff functions in many not-for-profit organizations. Just as there are many different types of staff, there are many staff stewardship roles: stewards as supervisors, as members of senior management, as line staff members, and as volunteers. We have to get the most from our employees, our volunteers, and ourselves. That's a lot, but if we use the overarching concept of stewardship—getting the most mission out of all of our resources—we'll go a long way toward becoming and remaining a stewardship organization.

We'll start with the role of supervision in a stewardship organization. You'll learn about giving up management ego, about management as a support function rather than a command and control function, and about how humility in leadership powerfully motivates employees and volunteers.

After that, we'll move on to the roles of specific employees in stewardship, starting with the executive director. He or she, like the president of the board, is in a make-or-break role for stewardship in the organization, so we'll review how an executive can be a better organizational steward. Then we'll follow the money again, this time examining the stewardship mind-set that your staff financial person needs. We'll set the framework for our longer discussion on financial stewardship in Chapter 7.

Next we'll look at the role of the management team and consider some ways to expand that team without hiring new people. And finally, we'll address line staff and some staff who unfortunately are often over-looked—volunteers. Both these important groups are key to mission success, and good stewardship demands that they be deployed wisely. But they are *also* stewards in the organization, with roles and duties to protect the resources of the community. In truth, everyone in your organization has stewardship responsibilities, and in this chapter, I'll show you the how and why. Sound interesting? Read on.

Supervision in a Stewardship Organization

First, a supervisor in a stewardship-based organization understands that the most crucial staff in any organization are those actually providing the service or making the product. (To accept that as true, the supervisor must have humility—one of the key characteristics of any steward.) The steward-supervisor's job is not to "boss"; it is to get the necessary resources in the hands of the line staff. As stewards, supervisors understand that management is, at its core, a support function, not one of command. Don't agree? Think about it. If you didn't have any staff to supervise, you couldn't be a supervisor. From now on, don't think of the people you supervise as "your staff." Think of yourself as "their supervisor."

Thinking like this turns the organizational chart on its head, and thus the moniker "bottom-up management." It's not new—successful organizations in competitive environments have practiced it for decades. It motivates staff and models stewardship values.

Being a manager in a nontraditional organization is a serious balancing act: valuing employees while keeping your authority, using your supervisory power while enticing employees to follow you of their own accord, making timely decisions while including as many people as possible in the decision-making process.

Rules for steward-supervisors

A steward-supervisor is really the not-for-profit version of the corporate world's bottom-up manager. Let's look at some relatively simple rules for the approach:

- The people at the line of service are the most important in any organization.
- Management is a support function.
- Push decisions (and responsibility) as close to the line as possible.
- Be as transparent as possible.
- Pass the praise, take the heat.
- Communication is about outcome, not process.

HANDS-ON

Tips and Techniques for Steward-Supervisors

Be of service to staff. At the end of group meetings, one on one meetings, or phone conversations with staff, ask, "Is there anything else I can do for you? Anything you need?" We all know (and you should tell the people you are supervising) that you can't give everyone everything they want: there isn't enough money. But you need to ask, for the very simple reason that there are some things you *can* do, and you have to ask to find out. These questions help you get the most out of people.

Communicate clearly. As you wrap up a one-on-one conversation, both parties should repeat back what they have promised. So I might say to you, "I agreed to get you the projections you need by next Tuesday at five o'clock." And you might say "No, I meant *this* Tuesday." We'd fix the problem *before* it occurred. Use a similar process as you wrap up meetings. At the end of each meeting, have everyone list out loud what they promised to do, by when. Correct errors quickly and move on. As long as the corrections are not judgmental in tone, this will work. Remember, you are trying to fix the problem, not affix blame. You'll be amazed at the improved attention in meetings and the quick drop in the error rate.

The people at the line of service are the most important in any organization

This rule contradicts American society's perception of supervisors, managers, and executives. Aren't people with more salary more important? Look at the way we describe this—we call it "top" management, or "climbing the ladder," or "getting to the top," all metaphors based on the traditional pyramid structure for organizations, with the most senior people at the small, higher end, and the entry-level people at the broad base, shown at the bottom.

But think about it. How many clothes is Nordstrom's going to sell without its excellent, motivated sales staff? How many packages will UPS or FedEx deliver without their great delivery people? How many rooms get cleaned, or meals served, or luggage carried by the managers at Marriott hotels?

The answer to all these questions is the same: hardly any. But in those organizations, not only does the product get moved and the guests served, but they get served *well*, and customer loyalty is built. And, not surprisingly FedEx, UPS, and Marriott are all organizations where the line staff *are not the highest paid*, but *are highly valued* by their management and *told so every day*. These companies walk the talk with their employees. Are their relations with their employees perfect? Of course not. But I know people who fly for FedEx who make less than their counterparts at the airlines and would never leave because of the sense of team and the sense of being valued.

Management is a support function

Earlier you heard a truth that is uncomfortable for many supervisors to hear: If you didn't have employees to supervise, you couldn't be a supervisor. In a very real sense they are not your employees, not *your* staff. Think of yourself as *their* supervisor, and you will have made a huge beginning in becoming a bottom-up manager.

Your job is to get the necessary information, training, tools, and time into the hands of the people you supervise so that they can do the actual work of the organization. You are their advocate in budget and management discussions. You are their coach, their teacher, their mentor. But like an athletic coach or an orchestra conductor, you succeed through the actions of others—*you don't play.* (Of course, many supervisors, and even some CEOs do, in fact, provide direct service either regularly or on occasion. If you carry such double duty, you still have to coach and support the people who provide direct service.)

This is a difficult realization to come to terms with for many former full-time players: we used to provide direct service, we liked it, and now we meddle with our staff and get in the way of their doing the best job they can. It's a tough transition, but essential to good stewardship.

Push decisions (and responsibility) as close to the line as possible

You've heard this before, and you may resist. After all, don't you as a manager have the title, the experience, and the responsibility to make decisions? Yes, you do, but you can't be everywhere at once, and you no longer have the all-important perspective of being on the line where service is delivered. Train your people to make decisions, let them make those decisions, and hold them accountable.

> FOR EXAMPLE: Guests of the Ritz-Carlton benefit from a long-standing policy: Any employee (janitor, housekeeper, bellhop, restaurant server) is authorized to spend *up to $4,000* on the spot to fix any guest's problem. This is pushing decisions down the line in a very real fashion. Employees share in the profits of the chain as a whole and from the individual hotel where they work. Thus, it benefits them to keep stuff fixed so that it doesn't break, and so that they don't have to spend money to fix it. Staff are trained in (and practice) making decisions about guest problems. They also review problems that actually arose every week in staff meetings, figuring out what the best solution was, and how to avoid the problem in the future. The result? Guests benefit from the policy even when nothing breaks, because the people at the line of service are watching out for their guests.

FOR EXAMPLE: The United States military, although an authoritarian organization, *really* gets the concept of the most important people in any unit being "at the bottom"—the grunts with the rifle "at the tip of the spear," as military people like to say. Everyone and everything is geared toward supporting that grunt, and everyone is told over and over that their own job is crucial to winning the battle, even if it is driving a supply truck or off-loading ammunition from a ship four hundred miles away from the fighting. The U.S. military also superbly delegates decision making to its line soldiers. American soldiers go into battle knowing how to make decisions if their officers are killed or their communications cut off. Lieutenants or noncommissioned officers know how to make decisions if they have to without going to their captain or further up the chain of command. This makes our military much more flexible, much quicker to react, and much, much more likely to win, since no battle ever goes as planned.

Listen to your staff, train them in how to make decisions, and then hold them accountable.

Be as transparent as possible

The more people know about your organization, the better. The more information they can see about plans, about services, and yes, about finances, the better. The more open you are the better. Period. Which is not to say that it is easy, or always personally comfortable, to be transparent. But it's the best thing by far for the mission, because open organizations are better at engaging their employees and volunteers than closed ones. If people can see problems, if they are allowed to review plans, better ideas usually result (not always, but usually).

Not all your staff will embrace this, or even care. But many *will*, and they will become more involved, more engaged, and have more ownership. And these staff will add their brainpower to solving the problems that vex your organization. In the words of John Chambers, the longtime CEO of Cisco Corporation, "No one of us is as smart as all of us."

> Open organizations are better at engaging their employees and volunteers than closed ones. If people can see problems and review plans, better ideas usually result.

Moreover, the more staff see and know, the less they have to be suspicious of and gossip about. Will this end office gossip? If only. But if you are up front and out in the open, gossip declines.

Transparency does not mean breaking confidentiality, particularly if it is legislatively required. It does not mean telling everyone everything you are even vaguely thinking of doing some time in the far distant future. But it does mean sharing financial reports, minutes of all board and staff committee meetings, marketing plans, and strategic plans. It means letting staff review and comment on new policies, and, in general, opening up the management team's discussions a bit.

This will occur naturally when you broaden your committee structure to include staff from all levels and all departments (see the sidebar Populate

Becoming Transparent

One way to open things up, particularly in large organizations with multiple sites, is to develop part of your web site into a password-protected, staff-only section. Have a link to this area on your home page, and include items like pictures of new staff, lists of birthdays, updates on funding or legislation, minutes of all staff and board committee meetings and of the board meeting itself, notices of upcoming meetings, copies of policies and procedures, and links to online education. Add anything else that aids transparency.

Then repeat this for your board. No sense in being transparent just for your staff.

For boards, include the names of the members of all the committees, the committees' jobs, and when and where they meet. Include a description of the main services you provide, an organizational chart with pictures of key staff, and again, minutes, policies, and news.

Read soon: *Open Book Management,* by John Case.* It's a wonderful compendium of stories from both the for-profit and not-for-profit sectors on organizations that opened their books and turbocharged their organizations.

* New York: HarperCollins, 1995.

HANDS-ON

Committees with a Cross-Section of Employees, page 84). With inclusive committees, information will get out and about, where it can do you more good.

Here are two perspectives on information. Both are true; pick one.

Perspective One: Knowledge is power. If I keep all the knowledge, I have all the power.

Perspective Two: Knowledge is power: If I share all the knowledge, we all get powerful together.

Which one sounds more like a steward to you? Which sounds more humble? Which sounds like someone who wants to be held accountable? Which one walks the talk?

Pass the praise, take the heat

Here's a crucial leadership test. *Situation 1:* The people you supervise have been doing amazing and productive work, setting an example in your community of compassion and effectiveness. The mayor drops by to congratulate you. Do you say, "Thanks, Mayor, I appreciate the visit. I'll let everyone know you came by" or, "Thanks, Mayor, but the people who really did this work are out in the next office. I'd like you to meet them." *Situation 2:* The people you supervise mess up, and mess up publicly. If the mayor calls to complain, do you say, "Mayor, remember the people you met when you came over? I'll let them know how you feel"—or do you say, "I'm very sorry, Mayor. My fault. I'll do my best to fix the problem immediately."

In both cases the second choice is the correct one for a leader who wants to motivate her staff and convey that she values them. As a manager, as a leader, you are responsible for the actions of the people you supervise. Yes, even if their job is the most important, you are still their supervisor. So a responsible manager takes the heat for the team, but passes the praise to the line staff.

Note: *Pass the praise, take the heat* does not preclude you from saying to staff, "I just had a call I *never* want to have again…What happened?

How can we fix this *now*?" Taking the heat does not mean that you protect your staff from taking responsibility for their actions with you. They should be responsible to you and be held accountable for their actions, inactions, or major mistakes. But outside your team, and certainly outside the organization, you are the responsible party.

Communication is about outcome, not process

Leaders who are stewards try to get as much mission out the door as possible using all the resources at hand. That means communicating clearly and effectively *the first time*, with a minimum of misunderstandings, second-guessing, and other frustrating delays. Such problems—and damaged relationships—occur because we often focus on process in communications and are so ready to assign blame. To counter, accept this fact:

It doesn't matter what *you* say. What matters is what *they* hear.

Get the ego out of communications. It isn't about you. It doesn't matter whether you communicated poorly or they listened poorly. In a stewardship organization, who's wrong (and who's right) doesn't matter as much as the mission. Here are a couple of practical ways to keep communication on track.

First, check. When we talk with staff, we often say things such as, "I need those reports by Tuesday at the latest, and I need them all on regular-size paper, got it?" And of course most staff, not wanting to seem inept, or to bother us, answer "Sure," even if they don't have a clue. Give people a chance to give feedback.

Second, communication is 50 percent technique and 50 percent trust—something we've already noted as key characteristics of stewards. To build trust, make sure you pay attention to the promises you make and follow through on them. If you tell someone, "I'll get back to you with a decision by Thursday," it's a promise. Keep it. And if you can't, get back to the person by Thursday to say "I know I told you I'd have a decision by today, but this stuff got in the way. Tomorrow for sure." What you say matters. What you do about what you say matters more.

What you say matters. What you *do* about what you say matters more.

To sum up supervision in stewardship organizations: The people you serve are the most important in any mission-based organization, but the people who provide direct service to those service recipients—your staff—are the most important employees. If you get this idea, if you embrace it, you've taken a giant step toward becoming a leader people will trust and follow, and a steward who will get the most out of the resource of the staff and volunteers.

Top Management Stewardship Roles

Now let's turn to some key leadership roles among the staff of the organization: executive director, finance manager, and management team. These positions are reasonably consistent from one agency to the next. However, don't assume that you aren't a leader if you don't have one of these titles. If you are reading this book, you probably are in a leadership position of some kind. So as you read about stewardship and the executive director, the finance director, and the management team, translate the advice to your own role. *Everyone* leads in one form or another.

The role of the executive director

Harry Truman famously said "The buck stops here." And for any leader this is true. Remember the third characteristic of a steward: accountability. Thus the role of the chief staff person is to support the mission and take responsibility not only for his or her actions but also for the actions of the entire organization.

As with the board of directors, there are dozens of management tomes that give very good advice and very specific lists of the technical duties of an executive director. Following are some overarching responsibilities that incorporate many of the more detailed tasks:

- Lead from the front
- Be the mission cheerleader
- Do a balancing act

- Be an advocate for other employees
- Keep current about the field

Lead from the front

You can't lead from behind. Leading means being out front—on issues, on mission, in enthusiasm, and in advocacy for mission.

We've noted that words are important, but that actions are even *more* important. The executive director, more than any other person in the organization, needs to pay attention to that. He or she is the most visible, most watched, most imitated person in the organization. In word and deed, inside and out, be accessible and be visible to staff, the board, and the community. You will be judged by your actions much more than by your words.

Leading from the front also means doing what you can to help out. Never be too proud (remember humility) to pitch in, doing the most menial task to help out in a pinch, whether it is emptying trash cans before a board meeting or making photocopies for a special event. If you truly are a support person, help your staff and let your other managers *see* you helping.

FOR EXAMPLE: Consider the executive director of four homeless shelters in a large metropolitan area. The shelters provide no food, just a warm bed, a warm word, and a cup of coffee. Each evening the shelter workers sign people in, and each morning they clear everyone out by 8:30 sharp, clean up (often a wholly unpleasant task), and get ready for the next evening. The executive has been at it for nearly fifteen years, and he still does one evening of intake and one morning of cleanup every month. He does this to stay close to the service, to refresh his understanding of what his staff deal with, and to keep his passion for his mission's mission (excuse the pun). Thus when he asks a donor for money, he can do it with real passion. When he advocates for the homeless, he can tell current stories about real people firsthand, not through a report from his staff that he read going into a legislative hearing.

This steward leads from the front. Think of ways that you can emulate him, whether or not you are the executive director.

Be the mission cheerleader

Whether paid employee or volunteer, line staff or senior management, service volunteer or twenty-year governing volunteer, *everyone* in the organization is a steward of its mission. But the executive director is the chief steward, and thus also the chief mission cheerleader. It is the executive's responsibility to make sure that both the staff and the board stay focused on the mission. If either begins to stray, it is the executive's job to get them back on course. The executive director needs to ensure that there are regular mission celebrations where personal stories of success are reviewed and applauded.

> It is the executive's responsibility to make sure that both the staff and the board stay focused on the mission. If either begins to stray, it is the executive's job to get them back on course.

Out in the community, the executive director becomes even more important in mission proselytizing. He or she needs to regularly remind the community of the organization's good works, how it is spending its funds wisely, and how well it is accomplishing its mission.

To do this well, the executive director must live the mission, be excited about the mission, remind him or herself about the mission all the time, and empower someone else in the organization to help if he or she gets distracted or tired and strays from the mission.

FOR EXAMPLE: One not-for-profit executive used to tape a bold-typeface, large copy of her organization's mission statement to her bathroom mirror so that it would be the first thing she saw in the morning and the last thing she saw at night. Over time, she got used to the sign and ignored it. One day her eight-year-old daughter asked what the sign on her mirror meant, and then told her mother that she could make "a prettier sign." She drew a new copy of the mission statement embellished with hand drawings, color, and pictures of people helping people. The new art was a great improvement, and caught the executive's attention—for a while. About two weeks later, the executive asked her daughter for another picture, saying she would take the first one to work to share with everyone else.

Thus began a tradition of a new sign every three or four weeks, first rotating to the mirror and then to the office, where it was displayed in various places for a few weeks. The executive was more focused, and the staff saw the mission afresh.

Do what you need to do to stay focused on your mission.

Do a balancing act

Back to balance as a stewardship skill. The executive director has to balance many things. Not surprisingly, the most prominent are recurrent themes in this book: money and mission, board and staff, funders and service recipients.

Money and mission. The executive director is the first line of defense in the battle for priority between money and mission that rages in every mission-based organization. To achieve a good balance the executive must weigh and measure the relative returns on investment, both mission and financial, gained from various services.

Board and staff. Visualize a not for profit as a teeter-totter, with the board of directors on one end and the staff on the other. The executive director is the fulcrum, bearing the weight of the entire organization and trying not to let either side dominate. Boards and staff, even when working toward the same mission in well-intentioned ways, often have differing, sometimes conflicting, priorities. It's the executive's job to sort priorities, resolve differences when possible, and otherwise bring the parties as close together as possible.

Funders and service recipients. The perspective differences between funders and service recipients are often both deep and wide. Service recipients know what they want, while funders often feel they know what the service recipients *really* need. Funders have the money, while service recipients want more, faster, better services. Ultimately, the executive is in the middle. It may seem that this is a no-win situation and quite often both groups are simultaneously angry at the executive. But by building long-term trust, by listening to both sides, by looking at outcomes first rather than process, the executive can bring the parties closer together.

Be an advocate for other employees

Management is a support function—even for the top executive. So get all your employees and volunteers the resources they need to do their job in the best manner possible within the limits of sound financial management. Talk to staff regularly about their needs, and advocate with the board and funders for staff needs, training, and compensation. Don't assume you know what they need—ask.

Keep current about the field

The staff should all be well trained, and the executive can lead by keeping current on the organization's field of endeavor. This is a stretch in large organizations, and there is rarely time for it in any organization. Nevertheless, the executive director needs to budget time and funds to continually learn from peers, staff, publications, conferences, and online courses. Only by keeping current—by asking, listening, and learning—can you hope to guide the organization along the most effective mission path. You can't choose between a new method and the status quo if you don't know what your choices are.

As you can see, the executive director has lots of responsibilities. It's hard work, and a lonely job. But there is help! And one person the executive needs to be able to rely on is the director of finance. Let's look at that role in the stewardship organization.

The role of the director of finance

The director of finance has one of the most important stewardship roles in your organization. As with your executive director, there are many names you may call this person: CFO, financial manager, financial director. Whatever the title, and whether it's a one-person office or includes staff of thirty employees, the stewardship role is consistently crucial.

The director of finance must have a complete understanding of the finances of the organization, including how to optimize its cash flow and how to meet the sometimes overwhelming reporting requirements that funders pile on. ("Magician" is another term one hears for the very best financial managers.)

As with the executive director and the board, there are some overarching responsibilities for financial directors:

- Manage the organization's funds to yield the maximum mission benefit
- Plan and monitor the budget
- Keep the organization on the straight and narrow legally
- Project and measure return on investment
- Report responsively

Manage the organization's funds to yield the maximum mission benefit

Return on investment. Return on mission. Maximum income, minimum bank fees, the lowest interest rate possible, keeping track of cash flow, making sure that invoices are promptly sent out and bills are promptly paid, planning the best debt strategy. All of these and a thousand other tasks fall to the director of finance. But the main theme of all of these duties is to make sure that, on the financial side, your organization is getting every single iota of mission possible from the money available.

Plan and monitor the budget

The budget is really the annual work plan put into dollars and cents. It is essential to develop a budget, not only because it is required by nearly all funders, but also because it ensures that the resources are available to do the mission that is contemplated during the budget period.

In Chapter 7, Financial Stewardship, you will learn the importance of the deep involvement of line staff in budgeting. The director of finance needs to fully endorse such involvement, as it makes life more complicated; it's easier to budget if only a few people are involved. But the organization is more aware and ownership is shared.

Once a budget is established, its implementation should be maintained by the finance office, which should report budget status to the appropriate staff at regular meetings. Again, this makes more work for the director of finance, but the work is well worth it for the organization as a whole.

Keep the organization on the straight and narrow legally

More than any area, finance is fraught with rules, regulations, required reports, forms, and filings. All of this formal accountability comes to rest on the shoulders of the director of finance. The stewardship issue here is simple: a mistake can result in spending valuable resources (time and money) on lawyers, in hearings, or even in court. And while the organization's accountant should catch some of these things in the audit, the financial staff responsibility is really to make sure that they don't get missed.

Project and measure return on investment

Remember that return on investment in your not-for-profit is critical; all expenditures should be viewed as investments in mission. For the finance director, measuring financial return should be pretty easy, even if the concept seems new. There are easy instructions out there on how to do it. Measuring mission is a bear, though. The director of finance needs to work with the program staff to set baselines and figure out ways to collect consistent information on this.

Report responsively

The final responsibility of the financial director is to report responsively, which means that reports go to the people in the organization in a useful format, on time, and with written explanation when needed. This is difficult. Often software won't accommodate a certain report request without added calculations—extra work on top of the usual. But reporting is a support function that needs to serve the people being reported to, not the people developing the reports. Communicating the financial status and projections of the organization, explaining the numbers to nonfinancial managers, converting talk about expenses into a pitch for more mission, and serving as the financial resource for the staff members

HANDS-ON

First-Rate Help for Your Finance Officer

You can use your banker as one of your financial advisors. Your banker must understand what you do, but first, you have to get to know them. If you don't already have an individual small business banker assigned to your account, the CEO and CFO should ask to meet with one at the bank. Give the banker the twenty-minute dog and pony on your *business*, not your mission. Show them your financials, your growth over five years, your financial, personnel, legal, and funding challenges, and the opportunities you face. If you have a significant number of businesspeople on your board, let the banker know who they are. Establish your organization's credibility as a business.

Then meet with the banker twice a year—at budget time and six months later. Talk business. Get their ideas on your budget and ways to finance your growth. Bankers want your business, but they hate risk, and they see many not-for-profits as risky. So if you establish yourself as a competent manager in the banker's eyes, you reduce the perceived risk and improve your chances of getting the loans you will need at less-than-exorbitant rates or fees (high rates and fees are there to compensate for a banker's risk).

Once your CFO has a good relationship with your organization's banker, develop an ad hoc team consisting of the board treasurer, your finance director, your banker, your auditor, and perhaps one outside financial expert. This ad hoc team should look at the following issues at least twice a year:

- The long-term plan of the organization and how it equates to numbers. How will growth be financed?

- How many days' cash should the organization have on hand? What balance sheet and other ratios should the organization monitor? What financial benchmarks should be used?

- What is the appropriate level and mix of debt for the organization? What can it do now to strengthen its position to borrow in the future?

- What technical financial steps can the organization take to reduce liability?

- How should the organization appropriately measure the financial return of various programs?

These are just some of the issues that this technical working group can decide and then recommend to the finance committee. But this is first and foremost a group that will help the staff financial director, and thus it is his or her responsibility to get it up and running.

"below" them on the organizational chart are all important components of good financial stewardship.

Those responsibilities are far too much for most people to do on their own. So get some help for your finance director, even if you can't afford additional paid staff. Hold high expectations for transparency, and expect reports that the remainder of the staff and volunteers can truly use. The finance director is, above all, support staff to the rest of the management team, never a financial dictator.

The role of the management team

The management team is the staff leadership. They have to chant the stewardship mantra the most often, and the more they exhibit the characteristics of stewardship, the more *other* staff will start to exhibit them as well. The management is, of course, one step closer to the line of service, but often not at the line. Thus they support the line staff and their direct supervisors, but also help advise the executive director on how to best respond to the community and how to best steward the organization's resources. Sometimes this can be tricky.

Here are some ways management can improve their stewardship:

- Talk mission
- Get out of the office
- Be supportive coaches and mentors
- Get input, make decisions

Talk mission

First rule: "Mission, mission, and more mission." As with board meetings, have copies of the mission statement on the table at your staff meetings. Celebrate mission successes at your meetings; tell success stories whenever they occur. When a person brings a set of choices and wants a decision, not only should you ask them, "What's your recommendation?" but add, "Which choice supports our mission more and why?" Bring mission into the decision conversation as much as possible.

Get out of the office

You may have an open-door policy, but there are still people who will never set foot in your office because they are convinced that if they do they will *die on the spot*, simply because you are "the boss." To solve the problem, get out of the office, wander around, chat, invite complaints, and encourage people to ask for help or to let you know what's going on in their lives.

Be supportive coaches and mentors

Earlier you learned that you should be supportive of staff, acting like a coach or an orchestra conductor. Let's look at that analogy a bit more. Coaches and conductors both decide a lot of things—what's played or what the play is, who plays, and the tempo of the game or the music. Both bring out the best in their players by encouraging, cajoling, fussing, or sometimes being angry. How coaches coach or conductors lead depends to some degree on their personality. But successful coaches and conductors all know that their success comes through the success of others.

Coaches and mentors teach, pass on practical wisdom, and, most helpful of all, show by their actions what they believe. (Hence some earlier ad- monitions in this book: if you believe in lifelong learning, and want your employees to benefit from it, you need to go to training. If you hold people accountable for their behaviors, do the same for yourself.) Finally, good mentors don't do things for the people they mentor. They teach or show them the skills, knowing that the skill isn't learned until it is used.

If your people shine, the mission gets done better, more efficiently, and more effectively; you look good; and you are a better steward. Just as with communication, it's about the outcomes and the outcomes come most directly from your staff—it's not about you. (Darn, there's that humility thing again!)

Get input, make decisions

As a manager, it is your job to explore options, make choices, and move ahead within your area of responsibility. The Stewardship Decision Tree on page 30, and the section titled Have We Consulted Appropriately? on page 34, describe ways to make decisions and reasons to avoid the consensus model often used in not-for-profits. One of the greatest management time and energy traps is trying to gain staff consensus.

FOR EXAMPLE: Suppose the management team (and your the leader of this group) has a choice to make. We have three options, A, B, and C. At a management meeting you ask all ten participants for their ideas, suggestions, and choices. You let everyone speak fully, and make sure that disrespectful comments from others are not tolerated. The choices are all acceptable, but the informal tally shows option A gets three votes, option B gets two, and option C gets four, with one person unsure.

HANDS-ON

Populate Committees with a Cross-Section of Staff

To push decisions and responsibility as far down the organizational chart as possible, make sure every internal committee includes staff from multiple levels of the organization, both vertically and horizontally—understanding that there may be practical size limits on some groups. But always look for members from all levels, not just from senior management. Vertically means at every level, including line staff. Horizontally means from every division of your organization or every department. Avoid the trap of using the same three to five managers plus a couple of others. Broadening your committees accomplishes four goals: 1) it shows that you value the input of every group in the organization; 2) it increases transparency; 3) it nurtures future stars, giving new people the opportunity to learn how to sit on or lead a committee; and 4) it brings *great* ideas and input from otherwise unavailable perspectives.

But don't waste people's time on committees. Ask standing committees to evaluate themselves annually—meeting times, duration, responsibilities, agenda construction, and agenda control. You'll be surprised—meetings can be shortened and made more effective as a result.

Your job is not to pick the highest vote-getter or spend a lot of time trying to convince everyone to agree; it is to combine all the information and experience and make the decision—and then ask everyone to support it. They can answer yes, they can certainly argue their position, and they can record their dissent—but at the end of the day, they need to support the decision or decide to move on. *Note:* It's a lot easier for staff to agree to support a decision if they are sure that you will bear the responsibility for the decision if things go badly.

Many people, particularly in the human services, have difficulty using their decision-making authority. Therefore they prefer the consensus model. But a steward makes decisions because forward motion is better than gridlock for the people the organization serves.

Volunteers as Stewards

Your organization may well be one that depends daily on its volunteers. If yours is a soup kitchen, you may have one or two paid staff who plan and cook meals, but utilize thirty volunteers a day to serve, clean up, and wash dishes. Organizations like Habitat for Humanity, Special Olympics, and Airlifeline could not do what they do without volunteers.

Other not-for-profits make scarce use of volunteers, either because of tradition, because of legal, liability, or service issues, or oddly enough, because of funding.

You may well ask, "I can see what stewardship has to do with board members and officers, since they have to make the big decisions. But other volunteers? What's up with them?" Fair question. And there are two real answers.

First, we need to ensure that if we use volunteers, we look at them as a valued resource to be used as efficiently and effectively as possible. *This means putting a lot more into volunteer management than most of us do now.* This means taking the time to match volunteers with jobs that they are qualified for; having job descriptions and written expectations of volunteers' actions, dress code, behavior, and attitude; and training, evaluating, supervising, and giving feedback to volunteers. Remember, a steward's job is to get the most mission out of all the resources the organization enjoys. Not just the easy resources.

Second, your volunteers need to catch some stewardship fever: they need to care for the resources of the organization as much as you do. They need to be reminded that they are taking care of the assets of the community. One asset—your reputation and goodwill—is something that they need to be the most careful with. Everyone is on the marketing team—and that includes volunteers.

> **FOR EXAMPLE:** The director of an organization told a story about her meals on wheels deliveries. Most of her volunteers were retired and able to deliver meals each day. The director had fielded a complaint about a particular volunteer who was extremely friendly, but far too chatty. Indeed, once the meal was delivered the volunteer stayed to chat so long that by the time she left, the hot meal was cold.

In such a case, training and supervision are needed. The volunteer's friendliness (a real asset for meal deliverers) had gotten out of hand. Some regular phone surveys about customer satisfaction would probably have caught this before it got to the point of a complaint. And a chatty volunteer might be very welcome *after* mealtime.

Of course, some training in advance would have helped too.

> **FOR EXAMPLE:** A few years ago, my children and I were at a wildlife sanctuary that provided volunteer interpreters. Our interpreter took our group of eleven people through the preserve, answering our questions, encouraging input, dealing with a wide range of knowledge levels from the visitors without talking down to anyone. She was, to put it simply, *wonderful*, and added both to our knowledge of what we were seeing, and to the experience itself. She knew about the preserve, the wildlife, the environment, and about where the bathrooms were and how to get back on the highway.

After our tour, we had lunch in a large cafeteria on the preserve and heard other people from other groups raving about their tours and their interpreters. Something good was going on. A week or so later, I called the director of the preserve and told her about our great experience and what I had overheard about other tours. The director was happy to hear our story, and then went on to tell me about their screening and intense training. They also evaluated their interpreters at least twice a year. When I asked what the motivation was for all that work, she said, "We early on realized that these people *were* the face of our organization to most of our guests. Even though we can't afford paid staff, that doesn't mean that our guests [who pay to come in] shouldn't get the finest possible experience."

Volunteers need to be carefully used. They are a valuable resource, but they are not "free" in any sense. For more information on volunteer management, check out the great books, workbooks, and web sites in the "Resources" section at the back of this book.

Recap

In this chapter on employee and volunteer stewardship, we've looked at the ways in which your staff—in particular your executive director, finance director, and management team—can be better stewards every day.

Before we dealt with specific roles, we looked at how supervision works in a stewardship organization. You saw that the staff who provide the services are the most important in any service organization, and ought to be told that, supported, and treated accordingly. A true steward looks at supervision and management as a support function rather than a power position. In delegation, communications, budgeting, and meetings, good stewards manage from the bottom, as these rules illustrate:

- The people at the line of service are the most important in any organization
- Management is a support function
- Push decisions (and responsibility) as close to the line as possible

- Be as transparent as possible
- Pass the praise, take the heat
- Communication is about outcome, not process

The key roles come next: the executive director and the director of finance. These two individuals must embrace stewardship and nurture it throughout the organization. For the executive director, this means

- Lead from the front
- Be the mission cheerleader
- Do a balancing act
- Be an advocate for other employees
- Keep current about the field

The finance director has a different, but no less important, list:

- Manage the organization's funds to the maximum mission benefit
- Plan and monitor the budget
- Keep the organization on the straight and narrow legally
- Project and measure return on investment
- Report responsively

Next we turned to the management team as a whole to look at management approaches that bring out the best in staff. The management team should

- Talk mission
- Get out of the office
- Be supportive coaches and mentors
- Get input, make decisions

Staff roles in stewarding the organization are just as important as board members'. Staff have day-to-day, week-to-week stewardship challenges. Good management stewards remind, coach, encourage, and motivate. Some days they do this easily and other days with resistance.

There is one more group that can enable (or disable) the stewardship movement in an organization. Those are funders, and their input into and roles in the stewardship journey are the subject of our next chapter.

CHAPTER FOUR DISCUSSION QUESTIONS

1. Do we adequately value our staff and volunteers, particularly those at the line of service? How can we be better leaders in this area?

2. Do we act "top-down" or "bottom-up" in our supervision? Can the bottom-up model work here? How can we better value our line staff and volunteers in ways that they will appreciate?

3. Given our budget situation, how can we provide more training to everyone, but particularly our line workers? What options are available in our community, online, or through nontraditional means?

4. What can we do to increase staff participation horizontally and vertically? Who are our future stars?

5. How can we make the organization more transparent internally?

6. Do we as managers "wander around" enough? Where can we find the time to do more of this?

7. Are our executive director and finance director using the practices in this chapter? What tools and resources can we get to help them be even better?

8. Is our decision-making process strong enough? Do we get input and then make decisions, or do we let consensus stall us?

9. How can we strengthen our use of volunteers? Can we utilize more? How do we develop volunteer job descriptions and evaluations? Who on the staff should be in charge of this?

CHAPTER FIVE   # Funders
as Stewards

Funders come in all shapes and sizes, from governments to individuals, from foundations to corporations. Funders can help or hurt stewardship efforts by the way they fund, by their requirements for outcome measures and reports, by the level of involvement they demand. In this chapter we'll look at the how, what, and why of funders' important role in fostering good stewardship.

First we'll examine the overall relationship of funders to mission-based organizations, then turn to the individual, and very different, roles of contractor, donor, and grantor. Each of these has unique ways of either helping or hindering stewardship efforts in a mission-based organization. Finally we'll explore recommendations for funders as they consider ways to help organizations be better stewards of their mission and resources. Taken as a set, these recommendations can improve the relationship between funders and the not-for-profits they assist. More importantly, they can enhance the ability of the not-for-profit to perform efficiently and effectively—a shared goal of funders and not-for-profits alike.

A warning is called for here. My strong belief about the relationships between many (not all) funders and many (not all) not-for-profits is that they are badly broken, and do not achieve their intended goals. As you move through the chapter, you'll read my strong feelings (otherwise known as rants) about the ways not-for-profits treat funders and funders treat not-for-profits.

Please understand: I know many people in both professions. They are good, well-intentioned people who strongly believe that they are doing the right thing, doing the best thing possible for their communities—that they are already great stewards.

But despite excellent intentions, I see a huge, chaotic mess of unintended consequences—consequences that reduce the effectiveness of funding, increase resentment between the funder and the not-for-profit, and ultimately reduce the mission outcome that everyone would like to see increased. There is no animus in these words toward any individual or group. We've all arrived here together, and together we can fix what's broken with the system we've created.

HANDS-ON

Share This Chapter with Your Funders!

The ideas and recommendations in this chapter are intended to help funders see their role in a stewardship light, and also to give them concrete actions to help not-for-profit stewards do *their* jobs better. The ideas are also intended to help not-for-profit stewards better understand the perspectives of funders. After reading these suggestions, consider giving a copy of this chapter to your funders, then sit down and talk about it. To make this easy, this chapter can be downloaded at no charge from the publisher's web site at the following URL:

http://www.FieldstoneAlliance.org/worksheets

Access code: W423Stw04

The Relationship of Funders to Mission-Based Organizations

The not-for-profit sector is the only segment of our culture in which people pay to join groups so that they can meet and gripe about their best customers. The groups? Not-for-profit state and national trade associations. The customers? Our funders. The people who send not-for-profits money are *not the enemy,* contrary to what many not-for-profit staff and boards believe. Yet at most of these conferences, significant time is spent discussing problems with funders.

Funders have their *own* misconceptions—that many, if not most, not-for-profits are staffed and governed by naïve know-it-all do-gooders who don't understand the complexities of legislation, are constantly trying to "work the system" to their organization's maximum advantage, and whine about any oversight that is required.

Sound familiar? Yes, of course it does. Sound healthy? No, of course it's not. Yet funders and not-for-profit organizations seem to be stuck in this loop of mutual resentment and lack of trust that gets in the way of progress and takes valuable time, energy, and focus away from the provision of direct services. Not efficient, not effective, not good stewardship. *Both* funders and not-for-profit organizations need to use a stewardship perspective: the financial resources they are tending are *not theirs* and must be tended in a manner that maximizes mission-effectiveness.

How can funders be stewards? Let's look at stewardship for each category: government funders, foundations, corporate giving programs, and individual donors. *Government funders*—government employees—are called "civil servants" or "servants of society." They should (and usually try hard to) take good care of the public's money and get the most out of it in terms of services. *Foundation staff* work for not-for-profits themselves, and thus are stewards of their organization's assets, trying to optimize the impact of the services they fund, be they social, medical, arts, education, environmental, justice, international development, or other worthy causes. *Corporate donors* are stewards for their owners, whether those owners are a family or a large group of stockholders. They want good works done efficiently and effectively. *Individual donors* are stewards of their money, certainly, but also of their vision for their community, their nation, or the world through their particular cause. All of these funders want to do good, but increasingly they want to do good *their* way, on *their* terms.

If funders are stewards of their own funds, how can you, as a not-for-profit leader, help them see their role as stewards of *your* funds too, without asking them to stick their noses in places they really shouldn't be? That's a challenge, and one we'll deal with later in this chapter.

First, though, we have to acknowledge a few facts about the relationship between funders and not-for-profits:

- Funders are buying services from not-for-profits, not buying shares in the organizations themselves.
- Oversight is appropriate. Meddling is not.
- Measuring outcomes is a good thing. A hard thing, but a good thing.
- It's the funders' money until the not-for-profit earns it. Then it belongs to the not-for-profit.
- Oversight and reporting are a cost of doing business for the not-for-profit, a cost that should be considered by the funder.

Funders are buying services from not-for-profits, not buying shares in the organizations themselves.

One overwhelming misconception about funders is this: funders are supporting community service organizations. They aren't. They are buying services: recreation, transportation, education, prevention, or intervention, among many others. But in most cases they are not "supporting the organization." (The exception here is those funders who are part of the much-needed movement to build not-for-profit capacity or who are funding bricks and mortar.)

The idea that funders purchase services is certainly not new: entire classes of government funding are called "purchase of service." Still, the more any funder—government, foundation, corporation, or individual—can believe that they are *buying services as a way of achieving their community vision*, the easier it will be for them to follow stewardship principles.

When the misconception persists, there is an understandable tendency for the funder to feel that they should "help" the not-for-profit make sure that they manage their money well. That help morphs into requirements and mandates that increase the expense to the not-for-profit *and the funder* (whose employees must now take time to oversee the organization), blur the lines of authority at the not-for-profit, distract both groups from their missions, and ultimately result in poor stewardship of funds in the form of waste.

Related to this blurring between funder as helper and funder as purchaser is the problem of fair price for services. Funders and not-for-profit organizations share the blame in this: funders often offer only to pay for costs, and not-for-profit organizations often charge only costs, or cost-plus. The notion of fair price as an expression of the value delivered—and as a means of creating a viable, sustainable program—gets lost in this blurry mess. The mess requires added oversight on the part of the funder and extra compliance efforts on the part of the not-for-profit, translated into higher costs for both. Worse, it robs the not-for-profit of the incentive to develop pricing strategies that allow it to perform its services with quality while making money. And, the not-for-profit needs to make enough profit to plow back into research and development to improve service, innovate, train employees, and otherwise run a healthy, sustainable business.

Once a funder takes a "We are in charge" view, there is also an inevitable slide into paying for *costs* rather than paying a fair *price*. This process, which would never happen with a for-profit, is instituted to try to keep the funder's costs low. In reality, it requires more oversight (and cost) on the part of the funder and more compliance (and cost) on the part of the not-for-profit. Most importantly, *it robs the not-for-profit of the incentive to develop pricing strategies that allow it to perform its services with quality while making money.*

Make money? *Make money?* Should a funder allow that? I would respond to that inquiry as follows: Allow that? *Allow* that? Who put the funder in charge of that decision? First, that's the job of the not-for-profit's board. Second, a not-for-profit not only *can* make money, good stewardship *encourages* it to make money so it can reinvest that profit in serving more people. A funder's decision to pay *only* for a not-for-profit organization's costs is a short-sighted policy that perpetually keeps the not-for-profit poor.

The concept of purchasing services does *not* mean that a funder simply gives money with no say in how it is spent. Far from it; many donors are very involved in oversight of money use. Put simply, funders should get what they pay for. But they pay for service provision, not for the right to oversee management.

> **FOR EXAMPLE:** A state agency (funder) goes to a local mental health provider and asks the cost of five hundred days of day care for a severely mentally ill population. The provider comes up with a cost. The funder agrees that it is reasonable, but then tells the provider that the agency will only pay 80 percent of the cost—the rest needs to come from the local community "to demonstrate community connection, involvement, and linkage."
>
> That same afternoon, the people from the same state agency go to Dell and order five hundred computers. Dell provides them with a price. Suppose the agency then said, "Well, we're only going to pay you 80 percent of that, since you can find the rest from your stockholders, or you can simply give it to us." This would be unheard of—and Dell would walk away.

Why do we accept the first example as normal, and snicker as we read the second?

Funders buy services, not organizations, which brings us to the next rule.

Oversight is appropriate. Meddling is not.

It makes sense that if funders buy services, they should get what they pay for. Requiring reports, mandating interaction (through site visits and

Stewardship encourages not-for-profits to make money, so it can reinvest that profit in serving more people. A funder's decision to pay *only* for a not-for-profit organization's costs is a short-sighted policy.

progress reports), and seeing outcomes are ways to demonstrate that the service was provided. But appropriate oversight can easily slide into meddling, unreasonable reporting requirements, and measuring things that are really none of the funder's business.

FOR EXAMPLE: In the early 1990s I was asked by the Illinois Department of Mental Health and Developmental Disabilities (DMHDD) to review its requirements for oversight of corporate configurations. The agency director had issued a new set of accountability requirements a few years earlier. Predictably, the service providers were upset and accused the department of declaring "mandates without money," among other criticisms.

I was not asked to review the entire set of accountability regulations, just those pertaining to related corporations, as I had done a fair amount of work in the area of corporate configurations to enhance mission-capabilities. I had heard the complaints of the providers, some of whom had been clients of mine, but had never needed to read the regulations themselves. Now I read them, read them again, read them a third time, and could not believe what I was reading. The state was requiring a ridiculous amount of detail and information on details that literally had *no* relevance to the services being provided.

To summarize mightily, let's assume you are a provider of services to people with disabilities, providing sheltered work environments, residential services, transportation, recreation services, and some testing for infants. DMHDD might well have only funded your residential services. But if you had *any* affiliated or subsidiary corporations (say, a foundation, or a not-for-profit setup, as required by law, for a HUD 202 project), you had to provide the name, address, phone number, and social security number of everyone on every board; the articles of incorporation; bylaws; audits 990s and so on, ad nauseum. Now these corporations had nothing to do with residential services, but you still had to submit the information. This was nuts. And remember, I was only seeing the corporate affiliate part of the regulations.

I asked the people who had written the regulations what had happened to merit this amount of paperwork and oversight. Had there been some grievous malfeasance by someone, perhaps a provider who had skimmed or hidden money in a corporation or had duped the state in some way? Their answer (to paraphrase): "No, we just figured that while we were rewriting the regulations we should throw this stuff in, since you never know."

You never know. Here was so much distrust of the providers (some, I am sure, merited by past deeds) that the regulators were willing to make a preemptive strike by asking for an absurd amount of detail. They were, in effect, punishing the 98 percent of agencies that were honest and forthright, anticipating the 2 percent who weren't. Were the costs (to the providers and the state) considered? No.

The good news: we got the regulations changed. The bad news? The change happened only after the next example hit the news.

FOR EXAMPLE: While I was working with DMHDD, another state agency—our welfare provider—was in the news, it thought positively. There was a story that the state agency's enforcement division had, over the past fiscal year, caught twenty-three "welfare cheats" and saved the state over $300,000 per year. I happened to be doing a retreat with some of the welfare agency senior management staff at the time, and I asked what the enforcement division's budget was. The answer? *Four point five million dollars.* So they had spent $4.5 million to save $300,000. Did it bother the managers that they were spending fifteen times what they were saving? "No," they said, "because you never know."

Now there is no question that we need enforcement and investigation as a preventive measure. I'm not so naïve as to suggest that doing otherwise would be good stewardship. But good intentions often get out of hand, and far too often the costs of oversight are not either measured or paid for.

Funders need to regularly step back and look at what they *need* to know about what they are purchasing, not what they may *want* to know about the not-for-profit. For their part, not-for-profits need to work with funders to accomplish a level of oversight that assures both parties that the funder is getting what it pays for and is a satisfied customer.

This is a long-term quest, one that will convert funders and not-for-profits from adversaries to partners. The people the not-for-profit is in business to serve will be the real beneficiaries.

Measuring outcomes is a good thing. A hard thing, but a good thing.

The old adage that you can't manage if you don't measure is true. You can't tell if one option is better than another if you don't try to measure its mission outcomes.

Measuring outcomes is important for another reason: funders should, more often than not, buy *outcomes,* not *process.* (Of course, particularly in the early testing stages of a new idea, new service methodology, or new way of improving a community, outcomes won't be available—so process may be what's purchased and measured.) For funders and not-for-profits, outcome measurement can enable funding based on expected outcomes—good accountability, which of course is key to good stewardship.

It's the funders' money until the not-for-profit earns it. Then it belongs to the not-for-profit.

Once you buy into the concept that a funder is purchasing services, this rule is much easier to accept. Funders can and should be very cautious purchasers of service. They should check references, look into past service histories, require accreditation when appropriate, and bargain for a good price. That's what any responsible purchaser would do. But once the service has been provided and paid for, the transaction is done. The relationship should end there, at least until the funder wants to purchase more services.

This is not to oversimplify the issue of outcome measurement or deliverables. Many not-for-profits provide services (such as prevention of illness) that are not only hard to measure, but are very difficult to tag with a beginning and an end. But there is a transaction going on here, not a marriage. It may be a *long* transaction, it may be unruly to measure, but nevertheless, it *is* a transaction. The reality is that the transaction gets obscured with lots of unnecessary stuff. For example, funders ask for audits *of the organization as a whole,* not just the expenditures for the services they purchased. Many federal contracts mandate that if any property was purchased with federal funds (even in part), such property is forever owned by the federal government. Why do not-for-profits put up with this?

When funders and not-for-profits accept their roles and responsibilities as *purchasers* and *vendors,* all parties will benefit: funders (including the taxpayers who fund government funders), not-for-profits, and the people who are served. For purchasers (funders), this will mean asking for specific outcomes and measuring them. For vendors (not-for-profits), it means they must either accept or decline an offer to sell a funder a service, and then not run back to the funder for more help every time something goes wrong—in other words, to plan and provide services better, not just chase the money.

This relationship already exists for many not-for-profits and their more progressive funders, but is woefully absent in too many communities. Moving toward such a relationship for all not-for-profits will greatly strengthen the sector and reduce the unnecessary expenditures currently obligated to unreasonable oversight.

Oversight and reporting are a cost of doing business.

Once a contract is signed or a grant given, whatever level of oversight the funder and not-for-profit agree to (even the meddlesome level) is a *cost of doing business.* Many for-profit firms have license fees, permits, waste management regulations, payroll taxes, safety inspections, and the like imposed by them by the government or by customers. While they may not like the added expense, they understand that it is part of the business that they are in. They factor it in, passing on the cost (or a prorated portion thereof) to their customers. Similarly, not-for-profits and their funders need to accept the agreed-upon oversight as a cost of doing business—and be sure that cost is *covered.*

Complaining about oversight after the contract is signed is, to be blunt, *bad stewardship*. Unacceptable oversight could be lobbied out of existence through your trade association, or renegotiated before you accept the money. But once you sign on the dotted line, just do the work.

For this to work, funders must recognize the costs associated with the oversight they demand, *and then pay for the oversight*. If the funder adds requirements (whether an additional audit, or a level of accreditation, or a level of expertise on staff), the funder should be willing to pay, in full, the cost of complying with that requirement—plus the not-for-profit's additional administrative cost of compliance with oversight, plus any additional margin the not-for-profit would typically expect to negotiate in a business transaction.

Let's look now at how funders can be good stewards as they try to press forward with their own vision of mission from their fund-providing perspective.

The Stewardship Roles of Funders

When asked, "What is the appropriate stewardship role of your key funders?" many non for profit board members might answer, "To give us more money—and get out of the way while we do our job." In fact, funders have a number of important stewardship functions:

- Provision of funds
- Serving as a clearinghouse for ideas
- Oversight and accountability

Provision of funds

Funders provide resources that not-for-profits can use to provide services. As noted previously, stewardship dictates that funders think of their role as purchasing services rather than providing funding. This role helps not-for-profits observe the rule "No money, no mission."

Serving as a clearinghouse for ideas

Funders offer more than just money, of course. Funders, particularly corporate, foundation, or government funders, nearly always have access to information about the successes and failures of service strategies in other communities. Funders may well have staff to research such efforts and to focus their funding accordingly. As a result, they have the ability to help not-for-profits be better stewards by avoiding the mistakes of others. Of course, funders should also encourage them to innovate and to accept that they will not always succeed. Then funders can pass information about successes and failures to yet more organizations. (More on this later.)

Oversight and accountability

This is a key role. In a stewardship sense, accountability is a very good thing. Almost all not-for-profit staff and board members are self-starting, high-quality, *very* hardworking people. Thus they set high standards for themselves. Yet accountability to others helps. You may share my own memories of my childhood: I worked to learn, and I worked for good grades, but I knew that I was going to have to hand my report card (good or bad) to my parents. Even with my self-motivation, the accountability was an extra—and necessary—push.

No, funders are *not* the parents of not-for-profits. But funders *are* customers, and should be able to see the results of what they are buying. So oversight and holding organizations accountable *in an appropriate manner* is a crucial stewardship role for a funder.

Stewardship in Relation to Contracts, Donations, and Grants

The type of funding provided influences the stewardship necessary for those funds. There are really three kinds of funding, with many variations: contracts, donations, and grants. Let's look at each.

Contracts

Contracts are the most "businesslike" of the three types of funding. A contract usually requires a specific set of outcomes performed in a specific manner with a specific population, and is normally a function of government implementing a particular statute. Until the mid-1990s, most government funding took the form of grants. Now most of it is contracts, and that is a good thing.

Stewardship considerations. Sole-source contracting reduces innovation and, in truth, accountability: if you only have one agency to contract with and you have to spend the money you were appropriated, you tend to let small problems, even medium-sized errors, pass. Moreover, only contracting for costs, or worse, only for direct costs, permanently hobbles the organization, not allowing it to grow, innovate, or serve more people without coming back for additional handouts, perhaps grants requiring matching funds!

Donations

Usually made by individuals and corporations, donations come in a variety of forms including cash, stocks, bonds, autos, computers, and clothing, depending on the needs of the organization. Donors sometimes give small amounts all at once, sometimes huge amounts over a long period of time. Donors are the largest funders of not-for-profits and, sadly, also the most common targets of scam artists.

Stewardship considerations. Donors need to be sure that the organizations to which they donate are both legitimate (that is, not scam artists) and well run (that is, likely to deliver effectively on the funds provided by the donor). This is both good stewardship of the donor's funds, as well as good stewardship for the community. It discourages scam artists and makes it less likely that legitimate but ineffective not-for-profit organizations will survive. Simultaneously, it encourages good, effectively run organizations.

Grants

A grant, traditional for foundations, is meant to be looser in both design and implementation than a contract. Since it is often intentionally less "businesslike," a grant usually offers more flexibility as a project progresses.

Stewardship considerations. Grants often require a great deal of funder attention, and this can result in the funder feeling entitled to see everything inside the organization and its governance, not just the outcomes of what they are funding. On the other hand, grants, particularly the multi-year variety, allow midstream flexibility that can be used to encourage innovation and experimentation in grantee organizations.

Funders play an important stewardship function in the entire not-for-profit sector. This has been the case for as long as there have been not-for-profits. Now let's turn our attention forward to what funders can do to encourage better stewardship.

Recommendations for Funders

What should funders do to encourage better stewardship, more efficient use of resources, and therefore more mission outcome?

Here are four ideas for funders that can improve a not-for-profit's ability to be a good stewardship organization:

1. Design projects to fund outcomes or processes, but not both
2. Measure outcomes, not the organization
3. Pay the price, not the cost
4. Encourage competition, and let innovation follow

1. Design projects to fund outcomes *or* processes

Funders must consider whether they are buying an *outcome* or buying a *process*, and choose to do one or the other, not both.

FOR EXAMPLE: A funder believes that a new method of addiction treatment will be more successful. It approaches one of its grantees and says it is willing to fund fourteen beds for a year in a treatment unit—provided the unit tries the new treatment method. That's fine, but in this case the funder is not merely *purchasing* fourteen beds. Rather, the funder needs to state clearly that it wants to see an experiment around a new process, and then find out what the costs of running that process and measuring its success will be. These costs will probably differ greatly from the cost of the beds: the rehabilitation center will need to train staff in a new process, change its evaluation system, work with its accreditation board, market the process to its existing referral base, and so forth. The trouble, of course, is that the funder may develop its budget based on the simple four-teen-bed formula, and the grantee is likely to try to "make it work" based on the funder's offer, rather than demanding the level of funds required to institute and measure a new process.

Funders should explicitly state what they want, but also be willing to work with their vendors (the not-for-profits) in designing a project that pays for the its own costs, its attendant administrative costs, a reasonable profit, and valid outcome measurements.

2. Measure outcomes, not the organization

Good funder stewardship as well as good not-for-profit stewardship requires that outcomes be measured. However, funders sometimes confuse measuring outcomes with measuring everything in the entire organization. Buy outcomes—and measure them.

There are three caveats to this suggestion: First, foundations that provide program-related investments (essentially loans in conjunction with or in lieu of grants) should certainly check out the organization's financials before making a loan, just as any lender would. Those financials should show strength, reasonable equity, and a steady profit (profits are what pays back loans). So knowing about the organization is a good thing.

Second, part of the outcome may require change in the organization, such as achieving a level of education, certification, or accreditation. Thus it is appropriate, in certain cases, to require either staff education or accreditation with the understanding that it is a reasonable cost of doing business.

Third, a private or corporate donor, particularly someone considering a large or long-term donation, should ask to see the organization's financials, as well as quality indicators such as accreditations, licenses, and so forth. Donations are really the corollary of investments in the private sector without the equity return to the donor. Donors need information in order to invest in strong organizations rather than weak ones.

3. Pay the price, not the cost

If funders buy outcomes, not entire organizations, it follows that they should pay the price, not the cost. The *price* includes direct costs, indirect costs, and a slight profit that allows the not-for-profit to reinvest in itself after the grant runs out. Profit builds strength, giving organizations room to innovate, grow, serve more people, and respond to market needs without going back to the funder for more money. Letting a not-for-profit make money is legal, ethical, good business, and good social policy.

> **FOR EXAMPLE:** The Javits-Wagner-O'Day (JWOD) Act requires the federal government to purchase a certain percentage of outsourced services and products from people with severe disabilities. Hundreds of millions of dollars every year are contracted with local not-for-profits nationwide who employ people with severe disabilities to do the vast majority of the work. These contracts, which are negotiated with such agencies as the Department of Defense, Department of Commerce, General Services Administration, U.S. Postal Service, and Department of Interior, have a 4 percent profit built in. Why? So the not-for-profits can afford the needed growth, pay back loans on equipment purchased to do contracted work, and so forth.

Every single direct cost has an indirect cost associated with it. Funding *only* direct costs is like buying a hot lunch for a disadvantaged school child and only paying for the starches, not the proteins; eventually the child will suffer from malnutrition. Similarly, funding only direct costs injures the not-for-profit, distracts them from service provision, and often causes them to hide real costs by shifting them between programs—deadly in the long run, as cost shifting makes it difficult to discover the degree to which programs are economically viable.

If funders bid out their work and ask for price, not cost, the price will stay reasonable (competition will see to that), and yet strong and healthy not-for-profits will include all their costs in their bids. If they don't, it's their problem, not the funders'.

4. Encourage competition, and let innovation follow

A funder that spends time with a service provider, asks for its perspectives, and then designs a set of desired outcomes will have much better success than a funder that designs a program and simply asks the not-for-profit for the cost of a project they have no ownership of, and may well feel won't work. Funders should spell out their desired outcomes specifically and their limitations more generally, and then let people get creative.

> **FOR EXAMPLE:** A funder wants an outcome of 10 to 15 percent fewer high school dropouts over five years (a very specific outcome) in three local schools. The funder may include some general limitations, such as no employment or service discrimination, but other than that it should be open to suggestions and applications. The methods that the schools (or community groups, or churches, or individuals) use to achieve the outcomes are open to creative, innovative people to propose to the funder.

When groups compete, they innovate. Some innovations work, and some don't, *and that's okay*. Funders need to encourage that innovative spirit. Competition for outcome-based grants will deliver innovation.

Bidding, of course, is hard if the funder has never done it before. Going "sole source" is easier, safer, and more comfortable, but it is less beneficial for the people actually being served and therefore not the best stewardship of the funder's resources. A funder should carefully figure out what it wants from a project, develop a way to measure it (often in conjunction with the provider), bid out the work, and measure the outcomes.

For many funders this requires a major change in process and in outlook, and such change is difficult for all of us. But the benefits listed *will* accrue when these changes occur, and the funder's role as an enabler of good stewardship will be better fulfilled as well.

Recap

In this chapter we looked at the stewardship role of funders. We examined the relationship between many funders and not-for-profits as it stands today, and then we reviewed some "realities" of funding:

- Funders are buying services from not-for-profits, not buying shares in the organizations themselves.
- Oversight is appropriate. Meddling is not.
- Measuring outcomes is a good thing. A hard thing, but a good thing.
- It's the funders' money until the not-for-profit earns it. Then it belongs to the not-for-profit.
- Oversight and reporting are a cost of doing business for the not-for-profit, a cost that should be considered by the funder.

We then explored the roles of contractors, donors, and grantors, and how they can be better stewards in each setting. Finally, we looked at stewardship recommendations for funders:

- Design projects to fund outcomes, not process.
- Measure outcomes, not the organization.
- Pay the price, not the cost.
- Encourage competition and let innovation follow.

The nonprofit sector can be seen as having three parts: board, staff, and funders. All of these roles are integrated and intertwined and can work to improve stewardship. The staff can't make stewardship policy decisions without board approval. Boards can set policy, but staff have to implement it. Funders can block risk taking, or encourage it. Staff can alienate funders or work with them to find common ground.

CHAPTER FIVE DISCUSSION QUESTIONS

1. On a scale of 1 to 10, with 10 being "fabulous" and 1 being "hideous," how would we rate each of our top 10 funders?

2. What can we do to work more with the 10's and less with the 1's? How can we encourage the 1's and 2's to move toward 10's?

3. Do we treat our funders as if we are selling them services, or selling them our organization?

4. How can we share this information with our funders in a collaborative way?

5. Should we seek more contracts, more donations, or more grants? Why?

6. Do our funders provide appropriate oversight or too much? Why? How can we help them look at us in a more appropriate light?

7. Are we surly about our resistance to oversight? How can we be better vendors?

8. Are we innovative enough? How does our funding encourage this or hold us back?

DISCUSSION QUESTIONS FOR FUNDERS

1. How do we currently view our relationship with our grantees? Do we perhaps claim too much ownership of the organizations themselves, rather than of our projects with them?

2. How do our grantees see us? Can we gain a deeper understanding of their perspectives through holding focus groups or one-on-one discussions?

3. Can we recast our funding and monitoring procedures to put less burden on our grantees while still being good stewards of our funds?

4. Are we adequately encouraging competition between grantees to foster innovation? If not, how can we do more?

5. Are we purchasing outcomes, or are we really supporting organizations? Does either viewpoint bear an internal review?

6. How can we better foster good stewardship in our own organization?

CHAPTER SIX   # Planning
Your Path

Planning is hard work. Planning is not direct service provision, so it's not a high priority for many not-for-profit managers. Yet taking the long look is good stewardship. And figuring out an organization's direction in difficult, tumultuous times is *essential* stewardship.

In this chapter we'll look at planning from a stewardship mind-set, starting with the stewardship opportunities presented by creating plans. We'll see the four really good results that can come from planning for your organization, ones that make your stewardship efforts easier and more effective.

Then we'll look at some goals that any not-for-profit with a stewardship mind-set needs to carefully consider as it goes about its planning efforts. These goals are not intended to be copied and pasted into your plan, but rather to get you thinking about your own organization's goals.

Next we'll examine the issue of outcome measurement that, oddly, has to start *before* you plan, and will continue through the monitoring phase of the planning process. We'll review why measurement is important, and offer methods and resources for this increasingly important area of management and stewardship.

Finally—and intentionally last—we'll get to a suggested planning process. It has eight steps, and is very adaptable to just about any kind of plan. These steps are a template from which to design your own process.

By the end of the chapter you should have what you need to begin (or get back to) your planning efforts. Some of your tools will be hands-on activities, but many will be rationales with which to motivate and lead your staff and board to do good planning.

Stewardship Opportunities in Planning

Ever since I wrote *Faith-Based Management*, I have done a lot of speaking to faith-based organizations about their management roles and responsibilities. Planning is, of course, one of them, and I quote two famous philosophers on the subject.

> *"For which of you, desiring to build a tower, does not first sit down and count the cost, whether he has enough to complete it? Otherwise, when he has laid a foundation, and is not able to finish, all who see it begin to mock him, saying, 'This man began to build, but was not able to finish.'"*
> — Luke 14:28–31

> *If you don't know where you're going, you'll wind up someplace else.*
> — Yogi Berra

Whether the apostle Luke or the erudite Yogi Berra speaks to you more, the message is the same—have a plan. It's good stewardship.

This is not to say that a plan will solve all your problems, or foresee everything Mr. Murphy can throw at you, but it is a start. There are four stewardship benefits of planning, all closely aligned with our stewardship mantra of efficient, effective use of resources in pursuit of mission. The four benefits are focus, community involvement, effective use of resources, and disaster avoidance.

Focus

More than anything else, planning should focus your board, your energy, your staff, and your money on pursuing mission in a particular set of ways. Many people resist planning with the excuse that it restricts their flexibility if the situation changes. They reason, "Plans are fine, but what if we put in all the work to write a five-year plan and then in two years everything changes? What then? We're stuck with the plan."

Of course, nothing could be further from the truth. First, if things do change dramatically in unpredicted ways, then you should make mid-course corrections. If you planned a driving trip to Denver on a particular interstate highway and found the road closed due to an avalanche, you'd take a detour (a midcourse correction in your original plan). This kind of amended planning goes on all the time in our lives, as it should in our organizations.

The goal of planning is not to create "restrictions" but to focus your work and resources. You *should* focus on deciding who constitutes your target service recipients, funders, referral sources, and community contacts. You *should* focus on what your organization does best and how to match that up with what the community needs most. You *should* focus on what changes are occurring in the local, state, national, and global communities, and how those changes will affect your target markets and your organization. You don't *have* to, of course. You can just plan to do more of the same. But if you use the planning process to focus, the organization can use its resources more efficiently.

Community involvement

Community involvement is perhaps the most underused benefit of planning. A few years before every U.S. presidential election, both the Republican and Democratic parties renew their efforts to have "a big tent"—to attract all kinds of voters. Similarly, the planning process can expand your tent dramatically. Through an expanded planning committee, a wide review of draft plans, and the use of surveys and focus groups as needed in your research phase, you can widen awareness of your plans, involve people in a way that gives them ownership without slowing the process down significantly, get great ideas, and often avoid previously unseen pitfalls as well. It's win-win-win.

But it requires you, the steward, to care enough to ask, to take the risk of distributing your draft plan, to listen to the comments you get back, and to open up your organization to simultaneous input and scrutiny. This can be difficult, but it benefits your planning process.

Effective use of resources

The combination of focus and community involvement will greatly improve the effectiveness of your use of resources. As you focus on doing what you do best for the people who need you most, in ways that best meet those needs, you will identify and discard things that you no longer do well, or that you do well but people no longer want, or that just no longer have enough mission benefit to justify the financial cost. Perhaps you have noticed a trend that suggests major program changes now to get ahead of the curve for later. Perhaps in the planning process you identified a need for better infrastructure—a more efficient office, more cost-effective software, better training for staff so that their time is more efficiently spent.

All of these activities are part of planning. All of these activities are designed to improve your efficiency and effectiveness in mission provision. Remember, no matter how good your grant writers are, no matter how much money your development staff develops, no matter how large a government contract you snag, you still have a limit on your financial resources, you still only have twenty-four hours per day per person, and you still have only so much time your volunteers, governing or service, can give to the organization. Stewards use these limited resources wisely, and planning can help.

Disaster avoidance

The final stewardship benefit of planning is disaster avoidance. Planning, if you let it, is a way of getting the long view and seeing problems before they crash into your organization. Before you can set five-year goals, you should be looking out at least that far at the threats and the opportunities facing your organization. This assessment and the resulting analysis can, in some cases, help you avoid disasters. In many other cases, the planning effort will raise the concern and identify the risk to your entire management team and board, so that you will have more eyes and ears discerning problems as events unfold.

> **FOR EXAMPLE:** I've been a private pilot since 1985 and, like all pilots, I'm required to take regular refresher training. Instructors constantly remind pilots that they are ultimately responsible for avoiding other aircraft, which sounds logical, but requires that the pilot do a number of things simultaneously, including watching the instrument panel (make sure the plane is on course, at altitude, and running correctly) and looking out the window in a particular way that maximizes one's ability to spot other aircraft. One instructor gave me an early tip: "Look at the horizon. If the aircraft is coming toward you and is below the horizon, it is below your altitude and should not be a threat if it remains there. Same thing if the approaching aircraft is above the horizon. It's above you and should be out of your way. But if it is on your horizon you may well have a significant problem." Then the instructor added, "Even though the approaching aircraft may be higher or lower than you are *now*, keep them in sight. *Things change*."

Thus I learned early, and am reminded every time I take a flight review, that taking the long view —all the way to the horizon—is a great way to avoid disaster. Think about it. The further off you can see an approaching problem the more time you have to avoid it. Spotting a problem the instant before a collision doesn't do you much good. When planning for your organization, you'll no doubt uncover potential problems on the horizon—and you're more likely to keep your eye on them and avoid them before they crash into you.

Some Goals for All Organizations

Certain goals make sense for any not-for-profit that wants to be doing good stewardship. You may already have achieved them, and if so, great! You may want to consider them, and reword them to have a different emphasis. Fine. In certain cases, they may be inappropriate for your organization—but please take time to consider them. They also serve as examples from which you can develop more fitting goals. The goals are

1. Become a market-driven, and still mission-based, organization
2. Become better stewards of our resources
3. Become financially empowered
4. Treat everyone involved with our organization with respect
5. Constantly seek to improve quality

Goal 1: Become a market-driven, and still mission-based, organization

Market-driven, mission-based organizations pay attention to what all their various markets want, and try to give it to them. They focus on customer service and customer satisfaction, making sure that they are constantly innovating and attempting to improve services in both small and large ways. They recognize that a good not-for-profit marketer works to make people *want* what they *need*.

Goal 2: Become better stewards of our resources

Stewardship organizations worry about good budgeting, monitoring, oversight, and outcome measurement. They measure return on investment and try to evaluate all their options. They have plans, and they use those plans to focus their limited resources as efficiently and effectively as possible.

Goal 3: Become financially empowered

Financially empowered organizations go for financial stability and then, when that is achieved, move past it into empowerment. They budget collectively, make money, use their reporting as a resource, are financially transparent internally, and have an endowment. They look at nontraditional income streams as the norm, and truly understand that while mission is first, without money no mission is possible.

Goal 4: Treat everyone involved with our organization with respect

Organizations that are infused with respect truly respect *everyone*—service recipients and customers, board, volunteers, staff, funders, external stakeholders, the community at large (which has granted tax exemption in return for some community good). This is both the *right* thing to do and the *smart* thing to do. For some organizations, this would be a value statement, not a goal. Others have some distance to go from where they are now to achieve this status. Be sure the goal is part of your organization.

Goal 5: Constantly seek to improve quality

Organizations committed to their customers typically seek to continuously improve their quality in all respects—quality of services, quality of employment, quality of volunteer experiences, quality of reporting and accountability. As has been said before by wiser heads, "The journey to excellence is never completed. There is always a bit further to go." Start the trip now and document it in your plan.

There are, of course, dozens if not hundreds of other goals to consider, ones that address the specific situations that confront your organization. That having been said, you do not need hundreds of goals in your plan. Most organizations that are successful both in their planning and implementation have between eight and fourteen goals. Some have as few as five. This means, of course, that you will have to winnow down the goals you come up with, but that's part of the process discussed at the end of this chapter.

Remember, the goals listed above are helpful, valid ones, but perhaps not ones that work for your organization. Consider them, but don't cut and paste them into your plan.

Outcome Measurement

You can't be a good steward if you aren't concerned about outcomes. Outcome measurement starts when an organization develops its plan. Many already measure outcomes because a contract or grant requires it, but a true organization-wide focus on measuring often starts in a strategic planning process.

There are excellent books, web sites, workbooks, consulting firms, and other resources on outcome measurement, some of the best of which are provided in the Resources section, page 233. But there are a number of stewardship and leadership issues surrounding outcomes that need review here.

First, the management team must fully support outcome measurement. If you say you want to have quality, but you don't measure the outcomes of what you do, if you talk a good line about everyone being on the quality team but don't share negative data, how can you expect people to get involved, get enthusiastic, even care about quality and outcomes?

> **FOR EXAMPLE:** An organization set a goal to "Improve customer satisfaction among all of our various markets" and so they started by measuring their baseline satisfaction, something they had never quantified before. It was a good idea, until data came back showing 37 percent of customers were somewhat unsatisfied or very unsatisfied.
>
> The management team had assumed that everyone loved them since no one complained—a classic marketing mistake. Management was so upset by this number that they refused to release the data to the staff, on the grounds that "it would upset them." In fact *not* releasing the information upset the staff, as they wondered what the heck had been found in the survey. Further, the staff were deprived of evidence that improvements were needed—and were loath to trust management, who now demanded changes without sharing the results.

When you measure, particularly when you ask people for their opinions and ideas on how to improve, tell your staff and board this: *Praise feeds the ego. Criticism feeds improvement.* When you do statistical or true outcome measurement and your data falls below your goal levels, it is a heads-up to find what isn't working and fix it.

FOR EXAMPLE: A fine arts organization board called me in when they were in a major crisis. The executive director had announced that they wouldn't make their budget numbers for the year. A number of staff had been laid off, some had quit, and the board hired me to help with the crisis. The organization's funds came from donations, fees, and foundation and corporate underwriting for particular events and showings.

I asked the board and executive about staff turnover. "Well, not too bad, but not good" was the answer. Not exactly measurable. That was the tip of the tip of the iceberg. They measured revenue but had no idea how many patrons or donors repeated year after year. They didn't even look at census counts of people who attended showings (which were required by the event underwriters). Questioned about the data, the executive said, "My job is to put art out into the community, not count the spoons in the cupboard every day before I go home."

It turned out they actually had most of the information they needed, they just didn't see that it was important. Recent data showed that staff turnover had risen each year for the past four years and, not surprisingly, the show census numbers were down, the number of donors had decreased, and the average donation per donor was down over the same period, in a straight, steady, alarming trend.

When all of this was shown to a staff-board meeting, the executive scoffed, "Well, it's easy to see this in hindsight, but no one could have predicted it." I disagreed and said, "This data shows four years, which is as far as I went back since that was when your budget problems started. I suspect that the donor and census problems started earlier, and that the budget problems are a result of the donor and census slide. And after the second year of information was available, you could have looked at ways to stop the slide. You had the data in hand. You didn't even need to spend money or time collecting it."

Figure Out What Counts—and Count It!

Get together with your staff and board and talk about measurement in general. Why is it important to your organization? How can it improve your mission? What difficulties will measurement bring—hurt egos or difficulty in tabulating and distributing data? Have this discussion early and get it all out on the table. Then, come up with five to eight factors that are really worth tracking. (Perhaps for you it will be more than eight, but start small.) You might measure new donors, occupancy, weekly revenue, or meals served—whatever is important to you and is relatively easily measured. Then establish a baseline. What are you doing now? How many, how much, how well? Start by finding out exactly where you are.

Discuss why the data is important and what happens that's good when the numbers exceed your goal. Then set improvement goals for these numbers: We will serve more than two hundred meals per week. Fewer than 3 percent of our counseling appointments will be can-

celled. Occupancy will increase from 50 percent to 70 percent over a six-month period. Set goals higher than your baseline! Raise the bar on outcomes.

Next, post the outcomes. Show the current data and the goal. Each week, month, or quarter, post the results. Make sure to explain carefully—to everyone involved in the goal—what the numbers, the goal, and the baseline mean.

Promptly discuss both successes and shortfalls to make any midcourse corrections that are needed. Be sure to celebrate your successes.

Note: Many organizations already have a number of outcomes to measure as a result of funder interests. *Be sure to share those outcome measurements within the organization.* Train people in what the information means, why it is important, and how everyone can help improve the outcomes.

Measuring needs to start at the top. This is a real leadership and steward-ship issue. You want to measure since you want to get better. Then you want to share that information, discuss results, celebrate successes, and fix problems early.

A steward works to get the most effective use of the resources at hand to accomplish the most mission possible. Measurement helps you increase both the quality and quantity of your mission work. It also helps persuade your funders to continue to support you. If you want your staff and board to support measurement, it starts with your leadership and stewardship.

A Planning Process

Now that you know why you should plan and have a leg up on some goals to consider, let's look at the "how" of planning. The process described below has been used successfully, with variations and improvements, for more than thirty years. The key outcome of this process is a plan that has wide ownership, diverse input, and is useable as a guide (rather than as a doorstop) for the board and the staff.

The process included here is mostly focused on strategic planning, as you will see from the examples. But the general framework is valid for all kinds of planning: marketing plans, disaster plans, and (with the modi-fications discussed in Chapter 8, Taking Good Risk) business plans. The process has eight steps that are adaptable and flexible to meet the needs of your organization. Just don't skip any steps. The steps are:

1. Prepare
2. Retreat
3. Research
4. Write
5. Review
6. Rewrite
7. Re-retreat
8. Adopt, implement, monitor

Get Your Terms Straight

Terms such as "goal" and "objective" can be defined in dozens of ways, but we'll use the following ones here. If you want to use others, that's fine, but come to some agreement about the terminology *before* you start the planning process. Don't use everyone's time trying to sort out a goal from an objective. Just agree to some terms. Then, *before* you start the process, perhaps as part of your readiness efforts, or certainly at the retreat, hand out a sheet that defines the following five terms: *mission* (and list yours), *vision*, *goals*, *objectives*, and *action steps*. Include some examples to make your definition clearer. It's fine to copy from this sidebar, if useful.

Mission: A short statement of the organization's purpose that explains what good the organization does, and for whom.

Vision: A verbal picture of the organization's desired future, usually a few paragraphs long; it answers the questions, "What will be different in the world in three to five years as a result of the work we do? What role will our organization play in creating that difference?"*

Goal: A goal is a broad statement of intended outcome. It may or may not be quantified, and may or may not have a deadline.

Objective: An objective needs four qualities: 1) it must support the goal, 2) it must be quantified, 3) it must have a deadline, and 4) it must have a named agent (a person or group) responsible for its implementation. Most goals will have multiple objectives supporting them. Those objectives can be sequential but are more often simultaneous.

Action step: An action step is the most concrete detailed implementation description. It may describe day-to-day or week-to-week activities. Like an objective, an action step has four parts: it needs to support its objective, it needs a deadline, it needs an outcome that is measurable, and it needs a responsible agent assigned for its implementation.

* Definitions of mission and vision adapted from *The Fieldstone Alliance Nonprofit Guide to Crafting Effective Mission and Vision Statements* by Emil Angelica (Saint Paul, MN: Fieldstone Alliance, 2001), 5, 7.

1. Prepare

Ready! Fire! Aim! An old joke to be sure, but one that has a lot of bearing on the planning process. If you start before you are ready to start, you can increase the likelihood of either not succeeding at all or of having to endure such a painful process that you never want to plan again. So make sure at least the following factors are in place before you start.

- **Enough time.** Planning takes time, lots of it. If you and your staff already have 2.6 Full Time Equivalents living inside each body, and you aren't going to get any more help, you might want to wait before adding one more thing to your list.

- **Enough money.** Planning almost always costs some cash, whether for retreat costs (if you go away), research costs, facilitator costs (a must for your retreat), and even smaller costs like printing and distribution of draft and final plans. Of course, people's time is also money, so budget time as well, as noted in the first item in this list. Make sure your planning expenses are in your budget.

- **Enough (and the right) people.** You'll need staff and board for sure, and you may want to bring in outsiders for some or all of the process. So line up the right set of skills to help you through the process.

- **A deadline.** Work expands to fill the time allowed for it. Thus, without a deadline, you'll never finish. In rough terms, most organizations take six to eight months from the time of their first retreat to adopting the final plan. Your timeline will depend on your yearly work cycle, vacations, and holidays, as well as on the amount of research you have to do, and your group's prior experience with planning. In any case, set a deadline.

- **An agreement on the kind of plan you are writing.** This doesn't mean whether the plan is a strategic plan or a marketing plan. Rather, make it clear that the product and the process are important to people, and that the result will be a better, more focused, more self-aware organization. Be sure everyone knows that the goal is to *use* the plan.

- **An agreement to measure before and after you plan.** You can't figure out how far you've come until you identify where you are. It takes money and time (and often delays) to get some baseline data before the plan is implemented, both of which are often resisted by board and staff members. So get agreement on measurement as part of Step 1.

Once you feel these things are accomplished, then you are ready to proceed to Step 2. But don't move on until you are really ready.

2. Retreat

The only worthwhile planning retreat locations are on beaches in the Caribbean. Really. It's a scientific fact that you get more done when your feet are on sand, as reported in the *National Enquirer*. Islands aside, going away *is* important, and it *is* a valuable step early in your planning process. Retreats allow you to focus on the organization as a whole, and really delve into its potential. They allow board and staff members to interact in a professional yet relaxed setting, and to share at length their perspectives on the threats and opportunities facing the organization that they all serve.

Here is what to consider regarding your retreat.

- **Get away.** Don't try to run your retreat in your office conference room during business hours, or even when everyone else is gone. It's too distracting and too normal. An off-site space emphasizes the importance of planning.

When time and budget allow, include an overnight. Here's one productive agenda: ask people to arrive at 6 p.m. for dinner, then work from 7 to 9 on "big think" items, followed by some social time. Have breakfast at 7 a.m., work from 8 to 2, then send everyone home. The overnight facilitates better socialization and a commitment to stay the entire time. It also allows you to do the hardest work in the morning when people are rested.

Require all attendees to take the same pledge: "I will be there for the entire meeting, and I will turn off my cell phone." Late arrivals, early departures, and cell phones are concentration and ownership killers.

- **Include the entire board and a lot of the staff.** Only in very, very unusual circumstances (or for more limited planning tasks, as noted below) should less than the full board take part in a retreat. You will need the entire board's buy-in later when you budget for the goals and objectives in the plan. You can use all the ideas you can get. Why *not* include the entire board? Another benefit—for most board members the strategic planning process is as deep into the organization as they ever get, and the retreat is the most in-depth immersion for them in the process.

  Staff need to be there (at least the management team) to provide their input and expertise. And of course if they have input, they have ownership of the product they will be in charge of implementing. The retreat also offers opportunities for staff and board to get to know each other better, a real advantage for any organization. In some planning situations it is not as crucial to have the entire board there. For example, if you are working on a new marketing plan, perhaps you would only include one or two board members: those on your marketing committee. And in that case you wouldn't include as broad a group of staff either. Be flexible, but don't pass on the chance to let people get away and really focus.

- **Get a facilitator.** Let's be blunt: don't try to facilitate your own planning retreat, and don't let another staff member, a board member, or a nongoverning volunteer do it either. Get an outsider who is skilled at facilitating and teach them about your organization and your issues. A good facilitator will learn quickly about your unique situation. They will also bring long experience in crowd control (often the most important function they serve), in pushing groups toward decisions, in keeping a herd focused on outcomes, all while reinforcing the importance of the process itself.

A facilitator also can bring some outside objectivity to the issues and, if they have worked for other organizations like yours, a wider sense of what others are doing to confront shared challenges. Look for a facilitator from your chamber of commerce, United Way, community foundation, or local management services organization. But get one and pay him or her. You will be happy you did.

- **Set goals at the retreat.** At the end of any retreat, you should walk out the door with a set of goals that can be incorporated in the plan. To generate goals, you need to analyze, brainstorm goals, and then prioritize them.

  First, analyze your situation. Ask the participants to go through a full or at least a modified SWOT (Strengths, Weaknesses, Opportunities, and Threats) review. If you don't have the time for the full SWOT, focus on the threats and opportunities. You can even just ask people what the biggest trend (good or bad) affecting the organization is, and what effect it will have. Start with analysis.

  Next, be sure the planning process generates some goals appropriate to the type of plan. Be sure the facilitator designs a process that involves everyone in goal setting, as this results in widespread ownership of the plan. The facilitator should also help you prioritize the goals.

  Finally, agree on the planning process for the period starting immediately *after* the retreat until the plan goes to its final adopting group (the board in the case of a strategic plan, the marketing committee in the case of a marketing plan, and so forth). State who will be doing the major work, list the deadlines, and note when the full board can expect to see reports, see the full draft plan, and adopt the final.

  You can get all this done in seven to nine hours of work if you have a good facilitator and if your group is no larger than thirty people.

- **Write it down.** When you get back from the retreat, make sure you write everything down: every goal, the prioritization process, the key points in the discussion, and, of course, the agreed-upon planning process. To the extent practical, let the rest of the staff see this report. Post it on the board and staff sections of your organization's web site and then e-mail people to alert them to its location.

The retreat should be a good communal kickoff to your planning process. Do it right, and you will really get the plan on track.

3. Research

For most goals, you'll require more information before a plan can be put in place to achieve them. For example, if people want to boost staff retention, you'll need to research what other organizations like yours are doing to hold on to their staff members. Or, you may have said you want to improve the satisfaction of your primary customers. To know whether you improve and by how much, you'll need to collect and examine baseline data.

The amount, expense, and time line for research vary from goal to goal and plan to plan. You'll have to figure out how much time—again, in people and in calendar days—you can afford for the research, as well as how much money you can afford to spend. But now is the time to get your facts straight, your costs of implementation estimated, your information gathered, to ensure that the goals and objectives you set are realistic, focused, and truly valuable to your mission.

4. Write

In Step 4, you draft the plan. The first draft of any plan needs to include the organization's mission, as the mission is the ultimate check against which actions must be balanced. Many organizations also include the vision, as this is sometimes more inspiring. Typically, the rest of the plan includes goals, objectives, and action steps—however, as you'll see in Step 6, it's best to write action steps only in the final draft of the plan.

Writing should start with the goals and objectives as set out in the planning retreat and then move to action steps. As noted in the sidebar Get Your Terms Straight, page 122, each objective and action step should support its goal, be quantified, have a deadline, and have a named agent responsible for its implementation.

Let's look at an example from an agency whose mission is *Assisting disadvantaged youth in employment and educational settings*.

Goal 1: Become more financially stable.

Objective 1-1: By the end of fiscal year 2005, the executive director and board president will develop a full-time financial committee comprised of staff, board, and outsiders to monitor our financial health.

Objective 1-2: By December 31, 2005, the financial manager will purchase and install upgraded financial software to allow better control, monitoring, and reporting.

Objective 1-3: By July 2005, the board president will have established a fundraising committee.

You can see that the goal supports the mission and that each objective supports the goal, has a deadline, is measurable, and designates a person responsible for implementation.

Some people choose to write action steps at this point. Because writing action steps is very detailed, it makes sense to write action steps *after* the draft has been reviewed and improved. This is part of Step 6.

5. Review

Now it is time for the community at large to get involved. You can't bring the entire board and staff, and all your funders, and all the people you serve, and all the key community players into every planning meeting. But you *can* involve them all, or at least give them a chance to be involved during the review stage.

When your draft plan is complete, print enough copies to be reviewed by representatives of all the affected stakeholders. This may include the full board, the affected staff, key funders, a sampling of people you serve (if appropriate), referral sources, and community leaders, depending on the type of plan and the scope of its impact. Distribute the draft plan with a letter and questionnaire. The following example is a review letter for a strategic plan; adapt it as needed to fit the type of plan you're developing.

[*Date*]

Over the past few months, the board of directors and staff of the [*Organization's name*] have been developing our new five-year strategic plan. We have generated our draft plan; a copy of that draft is attached. We'd love to have your input and have attached a quick response form and an envelope in which you can return it to us. Alternatively, you can e-mail us your input at [*E-mail address*], go online to complete the form at [*Web URL*], or leave a phone response at the following voice mail: [*Voice mail number*].

We believe that good planning is an essential part of our job as stewards of the organization. We hope that you will tell us what you think of our efforts and make any and all suggestions you see fit. Please respond by [*Date*] if you want our planning committee to consider your input in its plan revision efforts.

As always, we appreciate your support and look forward to receiving your input. If you have any questions, please call me at [*Phone number*] or e-mail me at [*Personal e-mail address*].

[*Salutation*]

Then enclose a form that asks at least these questions:

1. Overall, what is your reaction to our plan?

2. Which goal do you feel should have the highest priority? (please circle)

   [Include a list of the plan's goals here, so the reader can choose one]

3. Which goal do you feel should have the lowest priority? (please circle)

   [Again, list the plan's goals]

4. What goals do you feel should be added, if any?

5. Any other ideas, needs, comments, or suggestions?

Thanks! We appreciate your contribution to the plan.
Your ideas will influence the final outcome.

To solicit input from the staff and board, have a meeting or two to discuss the plan, answer questions about details and meaning, and take suggestions. You may also want to hold a community hearing on the plan if you have significant community-wide recognition. Then sit back and await the input.

Some of the ideas and comments you get will be great, some probably a little wacky. Regardless, list all ideas and comments on a chart like the one on the following page.

Reviewer	Idea	Staff Recommendation		
		Adopt	Do Not Adopt	Neutral
George C.				
State Agency	#1			
	#2			
	#3			
United Way	#1			
	#2			
Anonymous	#1			
	#2			

As you can see, you put the reviewer's name in the left column, any and all of their ideas in the next column, and staff recommendations on the right. The staff choices shown here are to adopt, not adopt, or be neutral on adoption, but you could substitute your own scale. Also note that in this example the state agency is shown having three ideas, and the United Way two. Putting different ideas on different lines lets the staff focus their recommendations on specific ideas, not on the total group of ideas from one reviewer.

6. Rewrite

At this point, you have lots of input, and may have gained information from other sources while you were waiting for the community feedback. After considering the new information, the planning committee should rework and complete the plan. If you are writing a strategic plan, the plan should be a five-year one, with the understanding that you will revise the plan in three years. If it is a marketing plan or disaster plan, use a horizon of three years. Whatever kind of plan you are writing, your goals and objectives should cover the entire planning horizon. Once you have collected community input, it is time to do some more detailed work.

For the work that will be accomplished in the first twelve months after the board adopts the plan, you should now add action steps. Without action steps—essentially, the work plan—implementation will not go smoothly. (Some organizations choose to add annual costs here as well, while others leave that to the budgeting process.)

Here's a continuation of the example started in Step 4, showing just the action steps connected to the third objective.

Objective 1-3: By July 2005, the board president will have established a fundraising committee.

Action Step 1-3-1: By January 2005, the board president will meet with the executive director to draft a list of duties for a fundraising committee.

Action Step 1-3-2: By February 15, 2005, the board president and executive director will select a chairperson for the committee, meet with him or her, and review the committee duties.

Action Step 1-3-3: By February 28, 2005, the fundraising chair and board president will meet to select other fundraising committee members from the board and from outside the organization.

Action Step 1-3-4: By February 28, 2005, the executive director will appoint a staff liaison to the fundraising committee.

The action steps support the objective of establishing a fundraising committee, specify outcomes, are measurable, and assign a responsible agent. You can also see that the action steps are much more detailed. In fact, this objective would probably include four or five more action steps.

This final plan should be printed and mailed to the entire board and any staff who came to the first retreat in preparation for your second retreat, described on the next page.

7. Re-retreat

Many great plans come unglued once implementation begins. Experience has shown that a *second* retreat can go far toward keeping implementation on track after a great planning process. A look at what you do during this *re-retreat*—particularly for strategic plans and new marketing plans—will reveal why you should do it.

The re-retreat should again include the entire board and the management staff. Have the planning committee chair briefly explain the process since the first retreat, and then walk through the goals and objectives one by one. This is tedious, lengthy, boring—and very, very important. This step forces all your board—some of whom won't have read or thought through the full plan—to review the full extent of the plan. Reading the goals aloud and talking about them ensures that every board member gets fully exposed to this very, very, very important document, and that no board member can later say "I didn't understand..."

While somewhat unusual, the re-retreat results in much smoother inter-action with the board during implementation, particularly around bud-geting adequately to fund the full implementation of the plan. And if serious concern arises about the content, the group can change, adapt, or modify the goals and objectives as needed. Better to go through this now than have the board or staff say "Oh, I didn't understand, I don't want *that*" six months into implementation.

8. Adopt, implement, monitor

This final step has, as the title implies, three parts. First the appropri-ate body, usually the board of directors, has to formally *adopt* the plan, then it should be duplicated and distributed widely. You might want to put some or all of it up on your web site; certainly your key goals and objectives could go there if they don't violate confidentiality or hurt your organization competitively.

Keys to Successful Implementation

It's a common problem: you create a great plan, and it either sits on the shelf or goes awry when implementation starts. Good stewards don't waste time on plans they don't intend to implement well. The following practices will help keep the plan on track:

- Prepare adequately by allowing enough time for careful planning, involving the right people, and setting a deadline.

- Be sure to have the plan adequately reviewed. Involve the people who oversee the plan, the people who implement, and the people who have a stake in its success. (They can be involved at different times—but do involve them.)

- Set objectives that clearly support their goals, are measurable, have a deadline, and name an agent (individual, team, or department) responsible for the objective.

- Develop a shorter-term implementation plan (usually one year) consisting of action steps for each objective. Paralleling the objectives and goals, each action step should clearly support its objective, be measurable, have a deadline, and name an agent responsible.

- Set up a system of regular progress reviews at management team meetings. Have the agents responsible for achieving the actions or objectives report on the progress, noting whether they are behind or ahead of schedule and what help they need.

- Provide a report for the board every three months that shows implementation progress, using both writing and graphics. Keep the board informed when you are doing well and when you are falling behind, as well as the reason for the deviation from the plan.

- Hold people accountable for their assignments. If you follow the process described here, everyone will have seen the goals and objectives in draft, seen the deadlines, and seen their names as responsible agents. Thus they have already had a chance to review and, if necessary, dispute the feasibility of finishing their assigned jobs in the time allotted. So hold them accountable.

- Be sure you've allocated enough money, time, and people to implement the action steps.

- Adjust the plan as circumstances change. Forecast a new implementation plan as the first year winds down.

- Unless confidentiality or loss of competitive edge prohibits you, make the plan public, and ask your stakeholders to hold the organization, its board, its leaders, and its other stewards accountable for the plan and its outcomes.

Then you need to *implement* the plan—actually do what you said you were going to do. Most organizations start to implement long before adoption: they've identified a critical need or issue and get going on it while the plan is still being finalized. This is fine as long as the activity is truly a high priority, and not just a management tactic to go around the process.

And finally, you need to *monitor*. Create an internal process to regularly review your progress toward implementation, whether you are ahead of schedule, on schedule, or behind, and to make adjustments as circumstances dictate.

This planning process has been used by hundreds of organizations—though everyone modifies it to meet their own particular needs. Don't let its flexibility lure you into skipping steps completely; you'll regret it. For example, organizations often skip Step 1 (Prepare) and Step 5 (Review). For Step 1, people don't want to take the time to get ready, they just want to get going. The result is poor stewardship, since you wind up wasting some of the resources you are committing to the planning effort. For Step 5, people either don't want to share their work or they are afraid of what "outsiders" (which sadly sometimes even includes their own staff) will say, so they pass on this step, using the excuses that it will take too much time or cost too much money. Again, bad planning and poor stewardship. You have the resources of the community's input, reactions, energy, and ideas. Why wouldn't you at least give that resource a chance to work for the benefit of the people you serve?

Planning is work. For most people it is not fun, not the highest priority nor the most enjoyable part of the job. But good planning, inclusive planning, long-range planning is good stewardship for all the reasons that we've discussed in this chapter.

Recap

In this chapter we looked at a crucial stewardship function: planning. First we looked at stewardship opportunities that arise from planning.

This is really the *why* of planning. What good things can and should happen when you plan?

- Focus
- Community involvement
- Effective use of resources
- Disaster avoidance

Next, we looked at some goals that should appear in plans in some form, though they will vary dramatically:

Goal 1: Become a market-driven, and still mission-based, organization

Goal 2: Become better stewards of our resources

Goal 3: Become financially empowered

Goal 4: Treat everyone involved with our organization with respect

Goal 5: Constantly seek to improve quality

Next we looked at the relationship between outcome measurement and planning—particularly measuring your progress in using resources effectively and efficiently. We reviewed some key reasons to develop baselines and to develop internal structures that support the regular reporting of information. You saw that first and foremost, outcome measurement has to start at the leadership level.

Finally, we walked through a flexible planning process that yields a well-stewarded, useful plan rather than a multi-page tree-killer. The steps in the planning process:

1. Prepare
2. Retreat
3. Research
4. Write
5. Review
6. Rewrite
7. Re-retreat
8. Adopt, implement, monitor

Planning is more enjoyable when you understand that it allows you to be a better steward of your resources. Ultimately, the people you serve will benefit—not just now, but far into the future.

Implementing a plan costs money, so long-range plans often result in a need to set your financial needs bar higher, and to figure out what the budget implications of implementation are, including short- and long-term capital needs, fundraising requirements, and staffing. That's the topic of our next chapter, Financial Stewardship.

CHAPTER SIX DISCUSSION QUESTIONS

1. Is our plan current? How and when should we begin the process of developing or renewing the plan? Are we ready, according to Step 1, "Prepare"? Have we freed up enough time, enough money, and enough people (and the right people)? Do we have a deadline, an agreement on the kind of plan we're writing, and an agreement to measure?

2. Who in this group has had bad planning experiences? What were they? How can we avoid repeating them in our planning process?

3. What should our planning horizon be? What horizon should we use, and what renewal cycle?

4. Who should be on our planning group? Any outsiders?

5. When we send our plan out for review, who should see it? Is there anything truly confidential or proprietary that we should excise?

6. How can we best coordinate our strategic plan, our marketing plan, our budget and annual work plan, and our capital spending plan?

CHAPTER SEVEN # Financial Stewardship

In many people's eyes, financial stewardship *is* stewardship. By now you know that it is much more than that. But there is no question that without prudent financial management, good stewardship is impossible. In this chapter we'll examine the key issues of financial oversight, planning, and monitoring, and learn how to look at them through a stewardship lens. This chapter will provide ideas both for financial specialists and for the more common nonfinancially-oriented managers.

First we'll explore some financial and nonfinancial reports that your organization must have and you must understand fully. These include cash flow projections, income and expense reports, balance sheets, and some ratios. You'll learn why it is so important to provide reports in context, and how to do it. We'll look at the best ways to generate reports that save the most time and provide the most oversight.

Then we'll turn to a financial decision process using our stewardship decision model from earlier in the book. We'll use the process with a number of real-life examples.

Next, we'll explore more thoroughly the concept of weighing two returns on investment, and look at some real-world examples of the dual return. This is a key element in stewardship financial decision making.

We'll look at the all-important areas of saving, borrowing, and investing in a stewardship organization. You should be saving, you'll probably need to borrow at some point, and as for investing—you'll see.

Finally, good stewardship organizations are accountable for what they do. In today's environment, that means they are *transparent*. We'll look at ways to become more transparent, and note some cautions about being *too* open.

By the end of the chapter, you'll have a great set of ideas and tools to apply to your financials right away.

Essential Reports for the Not-for-Profit Steward

As a steward—a board member, an executive, a manager—you need to know a lot about your organization's finances. But you also have other things to do, other issues that demand some of your daily twenty-four hours. If you spend all of your time obsessed with your financials, you can't be a very good steward.

First, a word about what to demand in all reports. There are three rules for making reports useful:

1. It should show data *in context*.
2. It should provide *accurate, complete information*.
3. It should be presented in a form that is *useful to the intended audience*.

Context

Numbers alone are not helpful. Reports should include useful background information, such as historical or comparative information, that provides the reader enough information to ask questions about the numbers.

FOR EXAMPLE: A surprising number of organizations provide financial data that doesn't really communicate because it lacks a context. Consider the following report:

INCOME

State	$12,500
Donations	1,250
Hourly Fees	21,450
Interest	1,110
TOTAL INCOME	**36,310**

EXPENSES

Salaries	$22,210
Fringes	3,450
Rent	2,400
Etc.	7,049
TOTAL EXPENSES	**$35,109**
NET FOR MONTH	**$1,201**

You can see that the organization generated a net of $1,200, but without a context, the figure is meaningless. Was the goal $120 or $1,200 or $12,000? That context alone would tell a better story—of problems, accurate forecasting, or perhaps a wild windfall. But without it, the numbers mean nothing. Even though the organization's executive and finance manager *know* the context, the report must show the context to all the intended audiences.

FOR EXAMPLE: Here's another report using nonfinancial indicators: occupancy, staff turnover, and the number of new donors per month. Which of the two displays is more valuable for a manager or a board member who sees the data?

DISPLAY 1

Indicator	
Occupancy (last month's average)	78%
Staff turnover (12-month average)	12.5%
New donors last month	23

DISPLAY 2

Indicator	Current	30 days ago	Goal
Occupancy (last month's average)	78%	76%	80%
Staff turnover (12-month average)	12.5%	12%	10%
New donors last month	23	20	30

Can you see how the additional context (history and goal) provides much more information of value to a manager in Display 2? The added context adds value and saves time: you focus energy on *why* there are variances rather than explaining that there are variances.

Accurate, complete information

Obviously, information is only helpful if it is accurate. This in and of itself can be difficult to locate and generate. Complicating matters is that, due to an organization's history and the sometimes bizarre constraints placed on it by funders, it is often difficult to track financial information back to individual programs.

A funder might say, "I'll pay for this program, but only for 22.5 percent of overhead." Or the funder might pay for overhead but disallow certain costs within that category, or require in-kind contributions of rent and insurance. These constraints kill the accuracy of many not-for-profits' program specific financials. To make the funder happy, the organization shifts costs around to make the numbers work, and reports the program costs to the funder based on this shifted accounting. After ten years of this practice for fourteen programs from twelve different funders, and after the people who made the original shifts have moved on, the program reports become *reality* rather than *adjustments*. So even if the numbers are accurate, they don't accurately describe the organization's programs.

The result of this cost shifting is that when the board and staff have to decide the financial return of a program versus its mission return, they can't do it well; they can't be good stewards *because they don't have accurate information*. They have cost-shifted information. They may be showing that program A breaks even when in fact it is losing money. They may be looking at a report that professes that program B is breaking even when it really is a profit center.

As you weigh the relative merits of a program, or of an increase or decrease in that program, you need to do it with accurate data.

Sit down with your financial team and review your programs. Look at any cost shifting you may have done and back it out. See what each program looks like when the true costs are allocated. Then ask your financial people to regularly (perhaps at budget time, perhaps quarterly) provide you with a program-by-program accurate look at your organization. (*Note:* Some organizations, particularly those with mostly earned income and donations, may not have this problem at all. But most do suffer from this problem to some extent.)

When you have reports that show context, and you are sure the reports provide accurate information, you can use them to judge the health of the organization and to make decisions.

Useful to intended audience

Thanks to today's software, a huge variety of reports—and reporting formats—are available. Be sure, when requesting reports, to follow this rule: *Give people the information they need in the format that makes sense for them and their role.* It makes no sense for a regular board member to see the financials in the same detail as the board treasurer. It makes much more sense for a staff person who oversees a particular program to have greater detail about that program, and general summary information about the organization as a whole. Target your reports so that their readers can make good use of them—and of their time.

How do you decide what kind of report is useful? A simple procedure is to ask the reader, just as you would any set of customers. For example, ask "How do you use the information you see now? How can it be made more understandable? How much detail do you need to do your job effectively?" Remember that any change in reporting will require the development of a good training session on how to read the new reports. Repeat this training at least every twelve months.

Now that we've explored what makes a good report, let's turn to the standard, minimum reports you need to see to provide good stewardship: cash flow, budget, ratios, and nonfinancial indicators.

Cash Flow

You need to know about cash—and far too few managers do. Cash is like oxygen: without it you die, and right quick. Stewards have to not only know their *cash status* (how much cash they have at any point), but also their *cash flow projection* (how much cash will come in and out of the organization in the near future). Both current cash status and cash flow projection can be shown in a single report. The forecast should go out six months, in monthly increments, and should show your projected receipts and disbursements (the cash equivalents of income and expenses) as well as a starting and ending cash amount.

FOR EXAMPLE: Here is a sample cash flow statement. Months are labeled 1-6 for simplicity, and both receipts and disbursement detail has been reduced from what your organization would have. The idea here is to get the idea!

	Month 1	Month 2	Month 3	Month 4	Month 5	Month 6
RECEIPTS						
State Grant	$12,400	$12,500	$—	$25,000	$12,300	$12,600
United Way	9,450	—	9,450	—	9,450	—
Donations	1,430	2,000	4,300	1,200	1,200	1,200
Hourly Fees	2,450	2,500	2,200	2,200	2,200	2,200
Loan Received	—	—	—	12,000	—	—
TOTAL RECEIPTS	**$25,730**	**$17,000**	**$15,950**	**$40,400**	**$25,150**	**$16,000**
DISBURSEMENTS						
Salaries	$19,550	$19,550	$19,550	$19,550	$19,550	$19,550
Fringe	3,519	3,519	3,519	3,519	3,519	3,519
Rent	1,320	1,320	1,320	1,320	1,320	1,320
Legal	—	—	450	—	—	—
Debt Service	—	—	—	—	860	860
Capital Purchase		—	—	15,000	—	—
Insurance	1,800	—	—	—	—	—
Telephones	246	250	250	250	250	250
TOTAL DISBURSEMENTS	**$26,435**	**$24,639**	**$25,089**	**$39,639**	**$25,499**	**$25,499**
STARTING CASH	$15,450	$14,745	$7,106	$(2,033)	$(1,272)	$(1,621)
RECEIPTS	25,730	17,000	15,950	40,400	25,150	16,000
DISBURSEMENTS	26,435	24,639	25,089	39,639	25,499	25,499
ENDING CASH	**$14,745**	**$7,106**	**$(2,033)**	**$(1,272)**	**$(1,621)**	**$(11,120)**
GOAL– 30 Days Cash	24,639	25,089	39,639	25,499	25,499	[5]

[5] This amount would be the expected cash disbursement for month 7, which is not shown on this graph.

Note that in this projection, the current cash status (Month 1) is fine, but there is trouble coming. Because of intermittent funding, and because of a capital project, the agency, even with some cash to start with, runs out of cash in Month 3.

The projection won't be perfect. It will be more accurate in the early months than later months, and it should be updated every thirty days. (Some organizations do this projection twice a month to reflect the impact of payroll disbursements. By projecting with twelve columns rather than six, they get a better idea of any real problems that might occur.) Accrual accounting covers a lot of cash holes, such as months when you earn money from the state but don't get the check. This kind of projection will help you anticipate that, and be prepared when cash dips.

Graphical cash flow projections

A graphical cash flow projection presents a quick view of the cash status. The graph below charts "ending cash" as the key line on the graph; each bar stands for a month. If you have already set a goal to keep a certain number of days of cash on hand, you can show that in the chart as well, and on the spreadsheet.

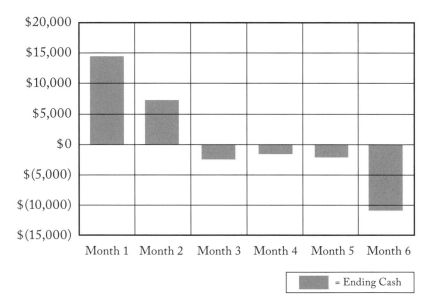

Budget

A budget is reflection of your work plan, showing where your income will come from and how you will invest your resources over some time period, usually a fiscal year. Think of a budget as a *contract between board and staff*—a contract that, once agreed to by both parties, should be monitored carefully. If the staff keep their part of the bargain and stay within the contract (the budget), the board should stay off their backs.

Sounds good, doesn't it? But this does not mean that the board should be cavalier about its budget monitoring duties, nor that staff should spend an inordinate amount of time on budget issues. You need to see regular reports on your budget implementation status, and you need to see them in a way that allows you to efficiently evaluate the budget status and raise questions if you feel that there are problems. The Eight-Column Budget Report, page 149, provides the necessary detail.

Look carefully at the budget report example. It shows a hypothetical agency's budget report to the board and staff. The key for easy use here is context. Let's look at the first four columns of numbers on the left. They reflect the previous month's activities. The first column shows "Actual" income and expense figures; the second displays the amount budgeted ("Budget") for each item. This puts the actual numbers in context. Then, in the third column, the math is done to compare the two. Finally, the fourth column offers further context by showing that variance as a percentage.

Moving to the four columns on the right, the entire report is repeated for the entire year to date ("YTD"). Why? Because every month is different. Thus one line item may be over or under budget for the month, but fine for the year as a whole—or vice versa.

Let's examine a couple of line items to see how this can work for you. Under income, look at State Program A. You'll see that this month the income from Program A exceeds the budget by $2,400. That's good. But slide over to the far right side and you'll see that this program is still behind for the year. The opposite is true for donations, which are 50 percent behind for this month, but up for the year over 250 percent.

This report helps stewards avoid obsessing over the actual numbers or even the budgets. Rather, stewards should run their fingers down the Variance columns and search for large problems—negative numbers in the Income, positive numbers in the Expenses. They should then check the year-to-date and see if that problem is also reflected there.

Hint: Some of my clients have a rule for board meetings: if the variance is less than 3% for a month, or 2% for the year, it cannot be discussed at the full board meeting—only at finance.

Another excellent use for this reporting format is with area, project, and division budgets. Here, the executive director can quickly review the projects and raise appropriate questions if the numbers are significantly off budget.

Remember, if you view budgets as a contract (between board and staff or between executive director and program managers), don't spend a lot of time asking questions when finances are functioning within the bounds of the contract.

Ratios

In finance, *ratios* are ways of simplifying complex numbers to make them manageable, and quickly and easily useful. Ratios may look weird at first, but they are incredibly valuable management tools once you understand them. Ratios are really no more than the decimal results of fractions, so don't be intimidated. They reduce really big numbers into digestible bites. With ratios, you don't have to look at your balance sheet too hard, which many nonfinancially minded stewards consider a great advantage. The key really isn't the math, it's the information behind the math.

One very common ratio is the "Current Ratio," which is calculated by looking at your balance sheet and finding two numbers: current assets and current liabilities. You divide the current assets by the current liabilities and you have the "current ratio."

Eight-Column Budget Report

LINE ITEM	Monthly Actual	Monthly Budget	Monthly Variance	% of Budget	YTD Actual	YTD Budget	YTD Variance	% of Budget
INCOME								
State Program A	55,400	53,000	2,400	4.5%	310,045	321,000	-10,955	-3.4%
State Program B	125,450	130,000	-4,550	-3.5%	767,890	780,000	-12,110	-1.6%
Medicaid	65,443	61,000	4,443	7.3%	422,449	415,000	7,449	1.8%
United Way	5,000	10,000	-5,000	-50.0%	30,000	60,000	-30,000	-50.0%
Fees	18,440	19,500	-1,060	-5.4%	114,598	124,600	-10,002	-8.0%
Donations	250	500	-250	-50.0%	10,500	3,000	7,500	250.0%
TOTAL INCOME	269,983	274,000	-4,017	-1.5%	1,655,482	1,703,600	-48,118	-2.8%
EXPENSES								
Salaries	105,800	107,900	-2,100	-1.9%	623,980	602,300	21,680	3.6%
Fringes	9,522	9,711	-189	-1.9%	56,158	54,207	1,951	3.6%
Occupancy	2,500	2,500	0	0.0%	15,000	15,000	0	0.0%
Insurance	8,000	8,000	0	0.0%	8,000	8,000	0	0.0%
Computer Expense	1,543	2,000	-457	-22.9%	14,345	12,000	2,345	19.5%
Interest Expense	234	400	-166	-41.5%	1,324	2,400	-1,076	-44.8%
Postage	879	900	-21	-2.3%	6,789	5,400	1,389	25.7%
Marketing	2,450	3,500	-1,050	-30.0%	14,356	16,500	-2,144	-13.0%
Utilities	1,244	1,200	44	3.7%	7,698	7,400	298	4.0%
Telephone	867	900	-33	-3.7%	4,680	5,400	-720	-13.3%
Depreciation	6,588	6,588	0	0.0%	39,528	39,528	0	0.0%
Supplies	2,240	2,500	-260	-10.4%	12,679	15,000	-2,321	-15.5%
Travel	1,243	1,500	-257	-17.1%	11,340	9,000	2,340	26.0%
TOTAL EXPENSES	143,110	147,599	-4,489	-3.0%	815,877	792,135	23,742	3.0%
NET	126,873	126,401	472	0.4%	839,605	911,465	-71,860	-7.9%

That's all fine and good, but you should be asking, "So?" The answer is partially in the definition of the term "current." A current asset is one that you can turn into cash quickly. Thus cash, savings, most receivables, equities, and so on, are considered current assets. In the ratio, these are weighed against current liabilities: debts that you might have to pay quickly, such as payables, short-term debt, and so forth. If current assets are less than current liabilities (generating a current ratio of less than 1.0), your organization could get into a serious cash crisis. Financial people would say, "The organization is not very 'liquid.'" The current ratio measures short-term liquidity, and it's something that you should pay attention to. If it drops below 1.0, that's bad. If it drops way below 1.0, that's really bad. If it rises too high, you may not be investing enough in mission.

If you agree that liquidity is important, isn't it easier to see a ratio of 1.25 than to divide $245,010 by $194,850? But as always, it helps to have the ratio in context.

What ratios should you monitor? This depends entirely on your organization, your cash flow, and the types and mix of income you have (grants, contracts, donations). Each kind of ratio looks at a different thing. For example, the *quick ratio* (*total* assets divided by *total* liabilities) shows your net worth; *debt-to-equity ratio* (total debt of all kinds divided by total net worth) shows how "leveraged" you are. Obviously if you have no debt, there is no point in monitoring debt to equity—but if debt is part of your world, you'd better attend to it!

Without deciding what ratios your organization needs—see the sidebar Get to Know Ratios, page 151, for advice on determining that—let's look at a couple of them as examples, and then some ways to use ratios in your stewardship. Your monthly financial report should include this month's ratio, last month's, and your goal. So your ratio report for this month might look like the table on the next page.

Monthly Ratio Report

	This Month	Last Month	Goal
Current Ratio	1.12	1.14	> 1.1
Quick Ratio	1.4	1.5	>1.4
Debt-to-Equity	.47	.55	< .33

This kind of report puts the ratios in a context that you can use. You look at the ratio's status, the trend, and the goal. If there is a problem, raise it. If not, you can be comfortable that your financial situation is stable, given the goals you have established.

Ratios can really save you time and keep you comfortable with your financial status. They will help you use your own time well, as well as the time of your board members. Give them a try.

Nonfinancial Indicators

Even though the topic of this chapter is financial stewardship, there are some nonfinancial indicators that need to be provided alongside the financial reports. Such reports help provide a better context for the

Get to Know Ratios

There are literally hundreds of ratios in the business world, but just a few that might be of use to you. Since your organization is unique, you have to figure out what those are. How? By talking to your financial team. Your CFO, your treasurer, your accountant, and your banker can probably come up with three or four that are really important and then set some benchmarks for you and your finance committee and board to use.

Suggestions of ratios to consider: current ratio (current assets divided by current liabilities), quick ratio (total assets divided by total liabilities), profit margin (profits divided by total income), and debt to equity (total debt divided by net worth).

HANDS-ON

financial data. The management team should decide which nonfinancial indicators merit reports. Usually indicators are important when they affect your income, your service quality, your expenses, or other key aspects of performance. Typical indicators include number of clients served, number of training participants, number of housing units provided, staff or client diversity, and so forth.

> **FOR EXAMPLE:** Let's look at some possible nonfinancial indicators by discipline.
>
> **Performing arts:** Number of tickets sold per performance, number of repeat season ticket purchasers, cost per seat per performance
>
> **Residential human services:** Occupancy percentage, employee turnover per month, referrals of new service recipients per month
>
> **Education:** Number of students, percentage of tuition paid by scholarship, new donors per month, percentage of alumni donations
>
> **Place of worship:** Congregants per service or per week, total offerings per week, number of volunteer hours donated per month

Choose three to five nonfinancial indicators whose monitoring by staff and board would help keep better track of your organizational health and help you see trouble coming.

Remember to put nonfinancial indicators in context, just as you did for your ratios. What's your goal? What's the history? What's the trend? Without context they are just ink on paper.

Good Financial Stewardship and Good Decisions

Now we come to the crux of the matter for many stewards. How do you make a decision when you are confronted with three or four different options? How do you choose between doing service A and doing service B, or worse, ending service A (which is bleeding you financially but important in service priority), or letting go three staff members who have nothing to do with service A? Or. Or. Or. Any not-for-profit manager reading this can recount dozens, perhaps hundreds of vexing choices his or her organization has been forced to make. These choices are always forced since there is always more need for your mission than there are resources to provide that mission.

So learning to decide, and learning to live with your decision, is a key leadership skill, and a *crucial* stewardship skill. In this section of the chapter we'll look at some ways to do better decision making, to better allocate your limited resources, to use a variety of people in the decision-making process, and still *decide*, then move on.

There are four things to consider in your financial decision making:

1. Include lots of people when you can
2. Budget in a big tent
3. Apply the decision template to financial decisions
4. Monitor and evaluate results of your financial decisions

Let's review them one by one.

1. Include lots of people when you can

You'll recall this axiom from our earlier discussion of decision making. Let's look at it in relation to finance.

> **FOR EXAMPLE:** You need to cut costs this year by 8 percent to make your budget balance. You have ideas on this, and so does your CFO. And you may well wind up having to cut staff. But you aren't at the line of service, and thus don't know where and how all your organization's money is currently spent. It makes sense to get all the savings possibilities on the table before you start to cut jobs and services.

The people in your organization are being asked to be stewards. If you are going to ask them to take on that role, they've *got* to see the numbers, be involved more in budgeting, be asked for ideas on ways to be more efficient. Asking for input increases ownership in making any changes mandated by the eventual decision. In the example above, it will be less painful to cut staff if all the staff know you have asked and listened to all the choices before you decided to reduce FTEs. They won't be happy with the decision, of course, and neither will you. But they will know that you asked and listened, and they will be *less unhappy* as a result.

Note that the recommendation is "include lots of people *when you can.*" Don't use that advice to procrastinate or interpret it to mean that "most of the time you *can't* include lots of people." The reality is that there are times when decisions need to be made quickly, limiting the opportunity for consultation. One way to include lots of people without having to involve each of them on every decision is to use a planning process (for a strategic plan or other purpose) that has been very inclusive, as described in Chapter 6. By going through this effort, you gain the input of people from all points of view, and establish priorities that can guide your financial decisions as you move forward.

Like so much else in not-for-profit management and leadership, this is an issue of balance. To the extent you can, you should include the ideas and input of as many people as possible. At the end of the process, though, it usually will be your decision. Thus, gauging the length of time allowable to make any decision becomes a balance of input and expediency, of getting ownership from others without letting that process hold you back.

2. Budget in a big tent

The term "big tent" is one of intended inclusion. Include all your staff and board in budget development. Make the tent as big as possible.

As we discussed at length in Chapter 4, you need to value the people closest to the line of service. In budgeting, that means giving them a shot at suggesting how to spend the money the organization takes in, how to reduce expenditures (as noted in the example above), and what priorities the organization should have. Not only do you get more input, you get more ownership, just as in the examples above.

More importantly with budgeting, however, is that you set the foundation with all your board and staff for greater understanding of how your organization works. You then can use the budget and its monthly reporting as one way to let staff know how things are going.

3. Apply the decision template to financial decisions

Chapter 2 presented the decision template below. Let's use it, in a revised form, for an example of financial decision making.

FOR EXAMPLE: A not-for-profit community organization has been asked by a foundation to vastly and quickly expand its counseling work for teenagers at high risk of becoming gang members. Gang abatement is a high priority for the organization in its strategic plan. Rapid expansion of the program will use up nearly 90 percent of the organization's hard-won savings and limit its ability to expand into its other priorities—job creation for single mothers and direct food subsidies through a food bank. Even though the foundation will cover all the organization's costs, the expansion's cost in working capital (that is, the money used to run the program before the first payment arrives) will expend 90 percent of its savings. Remember, growth always soaks up cash.

The executive, her staff, and the board look at two options: 1) invest nearly all their savings and more than all of their available volunteer and staff resources in a rapid expansion of their *top-priority* service; or 2) continue to grow *all* their priority programs more deliberately.

While on the surface this might seem an easy decision ("We don't want to use all our savings up in one area"), the service in question is indeed the top priority. It is the most visible work they do, the work for which they have won not only local visibility but state-wide awards. And there is the consideration that if the foundation is turned down, it might not return in the future. Is "a bird in the hand" better? After all, this choice wouldn't result in the organization losing money on an accrual basis.

The executive looks at the decision tree. She already knows that both options support the mission (Step 1) and both are priorities (Step 2), although the counseling expansion for teens at risk of joining gangs is a higher priority, as determined by her board in the most recent strategic plan. She wants to grow quickly, both to be responsive to her funder and also to respond to the needs of the community.

Brinckerhoff's Financial Decision Tree

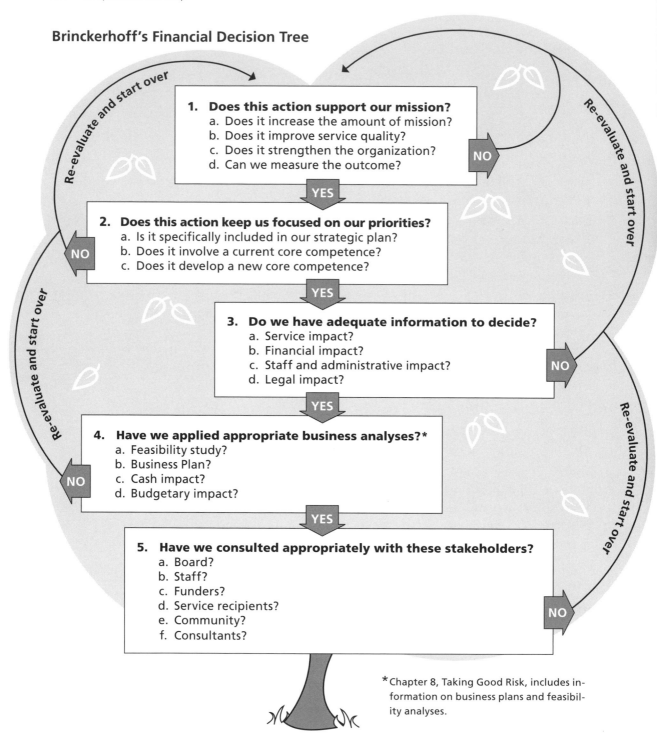

Re-evaluate and start over

1. **Does this action support our mission?**
   a. Does it increase the amount of mission?
   b. Does it improve service quality?
   c. Does it strengthen the organization?
   d. Can we measure the outcome?

NO

YES

2. **Does this action keep us focused on our priorities?**
   a. Is it specifically included in our strategic plan?
   b. Does it involve a current core competence?
   c. Does it develop a new core competence?

NO

YES

3. **Do we have adequate information to decide?**
   a. Service impact?
   b. Financial impact?
   c. Staff and administrative impact?
   d. Legal impact?

NO

YES

4. **Have we applied appropriate business analyses?***
   a. Feasibility study?
   b. Business Plan?
   c. Cash impact?
   d. Budgetary impact?

NO

YES

5. **Have we consulted appropriately with these stakeholders?**
   a. Board?
   b. Staff?
   c. Funders?
   d. Service recipients?
   e. Community?
   f. Consultants?

NO

*Chapter 8, Taking Good Risk, includes information on business plans and feasibility analyses.

She decides that to make a good decision she needs a full feasibility study of the impact of the rapid-growth option (Steps 3 and 4).

After the study is done, the executive confers with her board, her staff, and community groups. Most of these people—but not all—quickly realize that rapid growth may put the entire organization at serious risk. Even though she will face criticism for not ramping up her anti-gang work, she defers, choosing to do good work in many areas rather than grow in a manner she considers reckless, despite the critical community need. She made a very difficult, but good, stewardship decision.

In this case, the decision tree helped the executive make a good decision. She did not want to use up all her cash reserves on a program that will put the organization at real risk of failure.

You can use this decision template as you budget, or as you do contract analysis or develop your capital plan. It will help keep you focused on mission, and on accomplishing that mission efficiently and effectively.

4. Monitor and evaluate results of your financial decisions

Use the decision tree to the left as you wrestle with financial issues and resource allocation dilemmas. Also work to ramp up your staff and board capabilities with financial issues. Even so, while you will sometimes use these capabilities to make great decisions, sometimes the decisions won't be so great—and you often can't distinguish good from bad decisions for some time. Thus the need to monitor the results of your decisions. Monitor your outcomes, measure your progress, and reexamine your decision-making process. Ask yourselves whether you would make the same decision today. Ask: Where could we improve the process? Did we wait too long to decide? Did we include the right people in the decision? Once it was made, did we explain the *why* of the decision as fully as the *what* of the decision?

Report out information regularly, particularly financial information: it needs to be shared widely or it loses value. You've already seen some sample reports. And don't forget, just handing people reports does not increase their ability to monitor and give you feedback. You should have already trained your staff and board how to read your financials. Now you may have to train them how to read new reports pertaining to a particular decision and its outcomes.

Decision making is an important stewardship skill, particularly when dealing with money. But there is another issue that we need to overlay onto your deliberations—return on investment.

Mission and Money

Let's return now to the important stewardship role of balancing mission and money. Among for-profits, return on investment (ROI) is a classic business tool. *Return on investment* is an expression of how much money a given expenditure will return to the organization. It's a mathematical approach to weighing the relative advantages and disadvantages of competing options.

Among not-for-profits, money must be balanced against mission, so a simple ROI analysis isn't enough. So let's start by looking at an ROI analysis in a for-profit situation.

FOR EXAMPLE: A businessperson has two choices. She can invest $100,000 of company money in a new piece of equipment that will make the manufacturing process 10 percent more efficient, adding $12,000 to the company's profits per year starting next year, or she can invest $60,000 in staff training that will also improve efficiency, but only add $5,000 to the profits starting two years from now. What should she do? Let's look at what she is really investing, and what she is really getting back for that investment.

Option 1, the $100,000 equipment purchase, returns 8.3 percent in profit right away. Of course the equipment will wear out over time, and doubtless has insurance, maintenance, and energy costs to consider, but for the purposes of this example, let's keep it reasonably simple. So, Option 1 costs $100,000 but returns 8.3 percent on that investment.

Option 2 returns less profit in dollars, but also costs less. In fact, the percentage return on investment appears to be identical—8.3 percent—if you just divide the profit increase ($5,000) by the investment ($60,000). But remember: the profit increase doesn't show up until the *second* year, making the two-year return only half, or 4.15 percent *per year*. That's a vote against Option 2; it returns only half of Option 1. But this option provides several other benefits: 1) she does not have to obligate the entire $100,000, giving her an advantage against future risks; 2) she retains some flexibility, in case another opportunity arises; and 3) of course, she can invest the cash in an interest-bearing account of some kind, which returns may have benefit for the company.

Finally, the first option is in equipment, which can break or become outdated. The second investment is in people, who can leave and take their expensive education with them. Hmmm. And this is a relatively *simple* decision.

For not-for-profits, the issues are more complex. The financial side can be relatively simple, as illustrated in the example above. But add mission and things get complicated, emotional, and passionate very quickly. Let's look at a simple example of what happens as we add mission into the mix. Consider a family that has to make a decision about how to use a windfall sum of money. On the surface, this will seem like a straight financial issue, but then family issues (their mission side) get involved and it gets dicey.

FOR EXAMPLE: Mary and John are faced with a decision on what to do with $15,000 that their dear Uncle Ernie just left them in his will. Their choices, as they see them, are these:

• Pay down $15,000 of the principal on their mortgage, which is accruing a rate of 5.6 percent annually

- Invest the money in an insured money market account at 2.5 percent
- Invest the money in a mutual fund that historically has returned 11.4 percent per year for the past 8 years
- Invest the money in a tax-free bond that pays 4.4 percent per year
- Replace their major appliances (washer, dryer, stove, dishwasher, and refrigerator), all of which are nearly twenty years old and constantly breaking down
- Go on a vacation with their two children to an exotic locale

Let's put the choices in a grid and analyze a bit.

Choice	Financial Return	Family Benefit
Pay down mortgage	Reduces $15,000 at 5.6 percent	Will save money now to allow for college payments later
Invest in insured money market	Returns 2.5 percent in taxable interest, but is insured. Rate may rise or fall over time.	Safe, low worry, keeps options open for future opportunities
Invest in mutual fund	Historical returns of 11.4 percent per year, but not insured	Higher potential return, higher risk, more worry
Invest in tax-free bond	Tax-free 4.4 percent per year	Tax law could change, bond price could erode—some worry, but less risk than mutual fund
Replace appliances	Reduce maintenance costs, reduce energy costs	Fully functioning appliances a joy for everyone, saves some money, saves time
Take a vacation with kids	None. The money is gone.	A once-in-a-lifetime family opportunity

In this example, equate the family's financial return with your not-for-profit financial return and the family benefit with your mission return. If you just look at the financial side, the choice of a vacation is a nonstarter. The money is gone with no chance of a return on investment. Think of this as a not-for-profit program that *gives* service away. On the other hand, in sheer dollars the highest potential return may well be the mutual fund, but look at the negative effect on the family—higher worry from the risk involved.

This example shows that complex decision making is not foreign to you, and that taking many things into account is something nearly all of us have to do regularly. In the musical *Fiddler on the Roof* the protagonist, Tevye, has to make significant decisions throughout the story, often saying "On the one hand…but on the *other* hand…" as he tries to decide. In the example above, there seem to be a couple of dozen "other hands" to consider. This is true of many, if not most, major decisions.

Weighing mission return

There's no easy calculation for mission return, but it is important that you look at the mission return for various investments of staff and volunteer time, cash, equipment, and property. I know that this is not easy, but a good steward will make the attempt.

FOR EXAMPLE: A symphony only has so many concert hall dates, so many musicians, so much travel it can afford. Here's a real-life mission-return choice for a symphony board and staff. Remember this choice is essentially revenue neutral, but there isn't enough money to do both.

Choice 1: Have all symphony concerts during the season include a full symphony orchestra, but program no pieces that require chorus or extra musicians such as added percussion or a harpist. With this savings on personnel over the course of the season, a smaller ensemble could do some daytime concerts in local elementary schools. *Mission return: Four hundred to five hundred children hear live classical music performed by professional musicians.*

Choice 2: Add extra musicians and chorus for "grand evenings" of music at the holidays and the final concert of the season. Widely publicize these concerts in the expectation of selling out the concerts.

Mission return: The "grand concerts" attract an extra two- to three-hundred attendees who may become regular patrons in the future.

Which would you choose? Of course there is no "correct" choice, and in real life, there were union, financial, marketing, public relations, and scheduling issues to add to the vexing choice. Other factors that might influence the decision: Are there restricted gifts focused on one or the other choice? Does the strategic plan focus on one issue more than the other? Are there tactical public relations or fundraising advantages of one over the other?

Remember that a high mission return is the most important thing you can achieve. It means you do lots of high-quality mission for a reasonable expense. Don't, however, make the mistake of narrowly confusing mission return with productivity or other relatively simple measures. Mission return is complicated. Good stewardship involves looking at all the complicated mission returns and making the choice that best balances them for the long-term benefit of the community.

Saving, Borrowing, and Investing

Saving, borrowing, and investing are all strategies that stewards need to understand and use. Interestingly, the only condition under which all three should happen is *when your organization is making money*. Sound strange? It's not, really. And if you are ready to skip this part of the chapter since your organization is not currently budgeting to make money, I urge you to read it anyway, as I may well be able to convince you that making money is vital for a stewardship organization.

Saving

Saving is a discipline, one that exhibits stewardship in two big ways. First, it shows good sense in putting funds away for hard (or even harder) times. Second, it shows good leadership, showing staff and board that spending every dime right now is not good operating policy.

Setting Savings Goals

Payroll savings plans are popular because they take the pain and temptation out of saving. Learn from these programs and have the board set up savings policies. If you have a strategic plan and an associated capital spending plan, you'll have some targets to save for. Same with your target for days' cash on hand. The board should establish a policy that some percentage of all unrestricted donations go directly to your savings, whether in a building fund, an endowment (see below), or a cash savings account. If you need to—either to attract donors or to fend off funders who go after unrestricted funds like vultures— put some restrictions on the money. But a board policy on saving that is implemented first dollar, not last, makes the saving for the staff, and for the finance committee, much easier.

An endowment is one special type of savings that most organizations should start, and as soon as possible. Every endowment is started with the first dollar, yen, pound, or peso, so there is no excuse to wait for financial reasons. But you should think through the rules and uses of your endowment before you start. Having funds that are restricted in their use (a loose definition of the term endowment) is a good thing. It encourages long-term thinking by the board and staff, is a competitive advantage in soliciting donations ("Give the gift that keeps on giving"), and discourages funders from raiding "unrestricted assets."

Note: Most readers do *not* need to set up a separate corporation, with all of its concomitant expenses, to establish an endowment. All that's needed is a restricted fund, set up by a binding action of the board of directors. You may want to establish a separate corporation, for legal, political, or marketing reasons, but remember that the benefits of such a move need to outweigh the costs, and separate corporations always have a separate audit.

Some not-for-profits suffer under the mistaken notion that they shouldn't have any money in unrestricted funds—or that if they have two dimes to rub together at the end of the fiscal year, people may not think they are "needy enough" to merit donations.

Sadly, there are still archaic funders out there who demand that you "use it or lose it," and you certainly can't put those funds aside. But if you have a fundraising capability, or if you have some nontraditional income, you can, and you should, be putting funds aside. How much? That depends.

Start by getting your financial team together. Put together a group of board, staff, and outsiders, specifically your banker and accountant, to look at your cash flow and cash balances for the past three years. How low did cash on hand drop? How high did it rise? Then look at your budget for the next three years. Are you growing—which soaks up cash? Are you making big capital purchases—which soak up cash? Are you starting new programs—which soak up cash?

Work with these people to establish a number of things: First, how many days' cash should you have on hand? Days' cash is simply a calculation of how much cash you expect to go through in the coming year—cash, not expenses—divided by 365. Are you comfortable with sixty days' cash on hand? Ninety? Two? You would be amazed how many not-for-profits measure their cash on hand in minutes or even seconds. I had a client not too many years ago with a $20 million annual budget. Monthly statements and audits showed the client typically had between $1,250 and $1,500 in cash on hand. Rough calculations put that at about thirty minutes of cash. Not good.

Once you've determined how many days' cash on hand to hold, you need to decide how much of it to have in true cash and liquid securities like money market funds and certificates of deposit, and how much (if any) to have in a line of credit. (More on line of credit in the next section.) Remember to calculate the number of days of cash you need in *days*, not in dollars. That way, as the organization grows, the cash-on-hand number will grow with it even as the policy determining it remains relatively unchanged.

Borrowing

If your only experience with borrowing in your not-for-profit is to get you through bad times, you probably have a prejudice against the concept of borrowing: it means things are bad. In fact, borrowing can and should mean that things are good, that opportunities abound, that more mission is possible.

Let's look at rules related to borrowing and why it may be a good idea.

1. Only borrow when you are making money. Don't borrow when you are in trouble unless it is *absolutely* the only option. Debt is paid back through profits, not through losses or by breaking even. Ask your banker or your auditor. Loans are paid back by profits, so only borrow when you are making money.

So why would you need to borrow if you are making money? To do more mission. Let's look at an example and this will become clearer.

> **FOR EXAMPLE:** The county government comes to you and asks you to run a transportation service for seniors in your neighborhood. The government is willing to enter into a three-year contract with you for the service. The accessible van costs $54,000 and your organization has only $10,000 to invest. What do you do? Well, if you want to leverage the $10,000 into more mission, you can borrow the remaining $44,000 and start the service. But you should *only* do this if the contract makes you money, if the income *exceeds* the total cost of the service's insurance, salaries, fringes, maintenance, fuel, scheduling, interest on debt, and so forth. You should *not* do this if the contract only breaks even. Thus, if you are making money, your risk is reasonable and borrowing makes sense.

2. Borrow for as short a time as possible. This is simply good business, and many readers have, in the past few years, taken advantage of lower interest rates to refinance their homes and reduce the length of the mortgage from thirty years to fifteen or even twelve. Another option is to increase the size of your monthly payments to pay off debt faster. The faster you pay off principal, the less interest you pay.

3. Bid your major borrowing. You should have a primary bank with whom you do most of your borrowing, but big commitments like mortgages should be bid out. Banking is extremely competitive, and you are the customer. You're buying money, so bid your loans.

4. Have a line of credit. A line of credit is a preapproved loan that is designed to accommodate "seasonal cash flow needs." For example, retailers use lines of credit to help pay for their inventory in the buildup to the holiday season, paying it off after the first of the new year. Not-for-profits have seasonal needs as well, often related to a state or local budget impasse that results in no payments being made for the first part of a new fiscal year. Talk to your finance team about establishing a line of credit, and then develop good oversight policies to make sure that you don't borrow on it unless you really need to. Lines of credit are great, but they can act like a credit card and get you in real trouble if you are not disciplined about their use.

Investing

If you have an endowment, and if you are budgeting for organizational profit, you will have funds to invest. You need to mix risk and reward in the right measure for your organization. The rule is simple: the higher the return, the more risk. Your financial team should set up some investment policies and, when the amount of funds merits it, *hire* a financial advisor. Don't get your financial advice pro bono. Certified financial advisors are liable for their advice, and not charging actually voids their liability insurance in some cases.

Financial Transparency

It seems every day we read about corporations that are under scrutiny for "cooking the books" in some outlandish manner. Many a not-for-profit executive has scoffed at the "crass business world" without considering that the public (including the giving and volunteering public) doesn't just look at for-profits with skepticism, but at all organizations that have let them down in the past few years. Let us not forget the American Red Cross after September 11, the Catholic Church scandal of the spring and summer of 2002, and the United Way of America's self-inflicted wounds of a few years ago. In addition, economic downturns make people more wary of how they donate funds.

All of this means that you want to make your organization more transparent. You want people to be able to see what the organization is doing, how it is doing it, and where their donations and support are going. First, some definitions. There are two kinds of transparency: *contractual* and *voluntary*.

Contractual transparency includes all the things your funders and donors require. For most readers this includes an annual audit and management letter, various state and federal reporting requirements, programmatic reporting to a government or foundation funder, and any individual reports to large donors. Contractual transparency is, well, contractual: you've got to do it. But there are ways to do it more efficiently and effectively, which we'll cover in a bit.

Voluntary transparency includes everything else you do to make the community (including your board, staff, nongoverning volunteers, and service recipients) aware of what you do and how you do it. Many organizations are constrained by confidentiality issues as to how much they *can* disclose, by habits regarding how much they *want* to disclose, and by time and budget limitations on their ability to pay attention to this issue.

Let's look at these issues in turn.

Contractual transparency

Contractual transparency comes in many different forms. It may be the audit your funder requires. It may be access to all your books, even though a funder or grantor only provides 3 percent of your total income. It may be activity reports, outcome measures, site visits, oral reporting by phone, letter, or e-mail. It may require volunteer time or just staff time. But in all cases, by definition, you are required *by contract* to provide the reports. Thus, you have no choice. Contractual transparency is a cost of doing business, so don't view is it as a burden—and don't waste energy complaining about it. Here are some ways to ease the task:

1. *Before* you agree to a project, find out everything you will owe the funder in terms of reporting, when, how, in what format, and so forth. Ask about flexibility and the possible use of technology to ease the reporting burden.

2. Make sure you can comply with the requirements. For example, if your funder wants weekly cash expenditure reports and your accounting system can't handle them, tell the funder before you agree to do the work.

3. Once you agree to the funding tell your staff, and remind yourself, that you agreed to this, and discuss how you can comply with your contract in the most efficient manner. In any case, meet the deadlines. Late or incomplete reports raise questions about competence and about what's going on inside the organization.

4. Don't forget the information you owe your board. While it isn't truly contractual, think of it that way. Be transparent and forthcoming with your board, and they will be much more supportive.

Voluntary transparency

Your organization, staff, and board are stewards of a public trust. You need to be transparent in both finance and service provision so that the public can see the uses of its time, talent, and treasure. Additionally, you want everyone to feel comfortable asking you questions about your organization, which occurs as the organization becomes more transparent.

Transparency is also the smart thing to do. The more people see your organization, the more they will think about it, give to it, volunteer for it, and use its services. Transparency is good management today as it heads off pejorative inquiry and enhances public and community satisfaction with your organization. Remember that employees and volunteers count in this too. Make sure that they see a lot of information about your organization as well.

How can you be voluntarily more transparent? Try some or all of these.

- Scan your IRS 990 form and post it on your web site.

- Post on your web site all your policies for service, fees, reimbursement, and so forth.

- Regularly add new or different pictures of your services to your web site and your marketing materials.

- Speak at local civic clubs about what you do—and leave time for questions.

- Invite members of the community to tour your organization quarterly. Give them a tour, tell them about your service, then feed them breakfast or lunch. Don't ask for money, help, volunteer time, or anything else. Just let them learn about your organization.

- Post pictures of all staff with a brief informational blurb on your web site—particularly when those staff are the first point of contact for service recipients.

- Ask for input on your strategic plan: distribute draft copies to key decision makers in the community as well as to all your staff.

Assess Your Transparency

Start the discussion with your board and staff soon. Ask questions such as: How do people find out about us now? How do they learn about our services, our finances, our donations, opportunities to contribute, and so forth? If people come in and ask for our financial reports, what's our answer? If people want to attend our board meeting, or view service provision, what's our answer? What are our peer organizations doing to be transparent? What does our state and national organization have to say about this issue?

HANDS-ON

- Let all of your staff see all of your financials (with some training *before* you distribute them) to increase internal understanding of what you are doing.

Remember when you consider whether or not you should be more transparent that you are competing with others for donations, for volunteers, for staff, and for people to serve. People don't like to walk into dark rooms—they like the light on. People like to try on clothes before they purchase. Being able to see, touch, and observe makes people more comfortable. Organizational transparency helps with that comfort.

Recap

Financial stewardship is a focal point for good organization management, and one where a small mistake can turn quickly into a big one. Even if you are not a born financial manager, you do need to pay attention to money, you do need to understand your organization's financial structure, and you do need to monitor how the money is coming in and going out. This may not be even close to being enjoyable, but it is part of your job.

In this chapter, you learned about the basic tools and the basic outlook you need to be a good financial steward. To review, every financial report should

- Have a context
- Provide accurate, complete information
- Be useful to the intended audience

And you will need regular, accurate, context-inclusive reports on

- Cash flow
- Budget
- Ratios
- Nonfinancial indicators

Then we turned our attention to financial decision making. You only have so many resources, and thus you have to figure out how to allocate them. Where's the best, most effective place to spend our money, our time, our political capital? We looked at the following decision making guidelines:

- Include lots of people when you can
- Budget in a big tent
- Apply the decision template to financial decisions
- Monitor and evaluate results of your financial decisions

Third, we looked the dual return on investment—mission and money. We looked at the concept of return on investment and how to weigh mission return. Next we looked at three important financial tools: saving, borrowing, and investing, and when to use each—noting especially that the best time for these strategies (including borrowing) is when the organization is making money.

Finally, we covered the very important part of financial stewardship that includes both accountability and transparency. Your organization needs to be accessible in a wide variety of ways, through both voluntary and contractual transparency, and we suggested how you can start your organization on this path.

"Mission, mission, mission" is always first, but never forget that "No money, no mission" is a close second. Stewards are financially aware but not financially obsessed, leaving them time to manage the mission, time to innovate—and time to take good risks with confidence, the subject of our next chapter.

CHAPTER SEVEN DISCUSSION QUESTIONS

1. Do we shift costs? How much does it affect our perception of our various programs? Can we develop information that weeds out the cost shifts?

2. Are we seeing the right information? Do we include enough context in our reports?

3. Are our cash projections accurate enough? How can we improve them?

4. How can we train more staff in better understanding our financial reports and financial situation?

5. What ratios should we be examining monthly?

6. What nonfinancial indicators should we use?

7. Can we use the Eight-Column Budget Report in our monthly financial reports? What about having differentiated reports for different groups?

8. How can we apply the financial decision template to our budgeting process?

9. Are we complying with all of our contractual transparency requirements? If not, how can we improve compliance?

10. How can we improve our voluntary transparency? What can we do online? With our staff? With our board?

CHAPTER EIGHT Taking
Good Risk

Why would a steward, who is managing someone else's resources, take a risk? Isn't safety
a better path? How could taking risks be good stewardship? But in fact,
we all take risks all the time. Consider money: even the most conservative investments are risky, and the more risk you take, the more generous
the gain or punishing the loss.

Stewards are investing all the time. They invest the organization's money
in the bank, in buildings, in bonds, in staff—and in the people of the
community. Stewards are really *social entrepreneurs,* looking to get the
most "mission return" on the resources they have at their disposal—
money, time, volunteers, and goodwill. Good stewards determine which
risks are reasonable ones to take with the resources the community has
given. *All* investments entail risk—but they must be made, because the
only way your organization can grow, innovate, or provide higher quality
services is through taking risks.

As a steward you can stay home and do only the "safe" things, or step out,
and learn how to take good risks. Remember, the corollary of "It's not
your stuff" is "It's not your outcome." If you as a staff or board member
choose to not grow at all, ever—and thus take no risk—do you suffer?
Not really, *but the people you serve certainly do.*

This chapter helps you learn to take good risks as a part of your duty of
stewardship. First we'll look at a social entrepreneur's decision-making

process. Then we'll look at risk reduction tools, specifically feasibility studies and business plans. Such tools are designed to help you evaluate ideas and ensure that you and your board fully understand the risks you are taking. In many cases, these tools will help you decide *not* to take on a risk, and we'll look at a number of examples to help you understand this better. Finally we'll look at the mission outcomes of taking risk.

The Social Entrepreneur's Decision Process

A *social entrepreneur* is a person who takes risk on behalf of the people his or her organization serves.[6]

This is a very, very good fit for a steward. If it's not your stuff, your risks are taken for the benefit of others. Look at it another way: for-profit entrepreneurs take risk on behalf of themselves and their *stock*holders; not-for-profit social entrepreneurs take risk on behalf of their *stake*holders.

And the decision process for a social entrepreneur looks like that used by stewards. You will remember the process on the next page from Chapter 2. Consider the "action" being discussed as a new or expanded service, or the start of a business, or entering a partnership, and note the addition of item 4-e on risk. With these adaptations, the process fits a social entrepreneurship mind-set.

So what we see on the chart is that the stewardship and the social entrepreneurship decision models are the same, but that risk becomes a distinct element of the matrix for the entrepreneur. Risk is fine, but stewards must always aim for mission outcomes while risking as little as possible.

How to do that is really pretty straightforward. We use a technique that has been used successfully countless times before: *business planning*.

---

[6] Peter Brinckerhoff, *Mission-Based Management: Leading Your Not-for-Profit into the 21st Century*, 1st ed. (Dillon, CO: Alpine Guild, 1994), 27.

Brinckerhoff's Risk Decision Tree

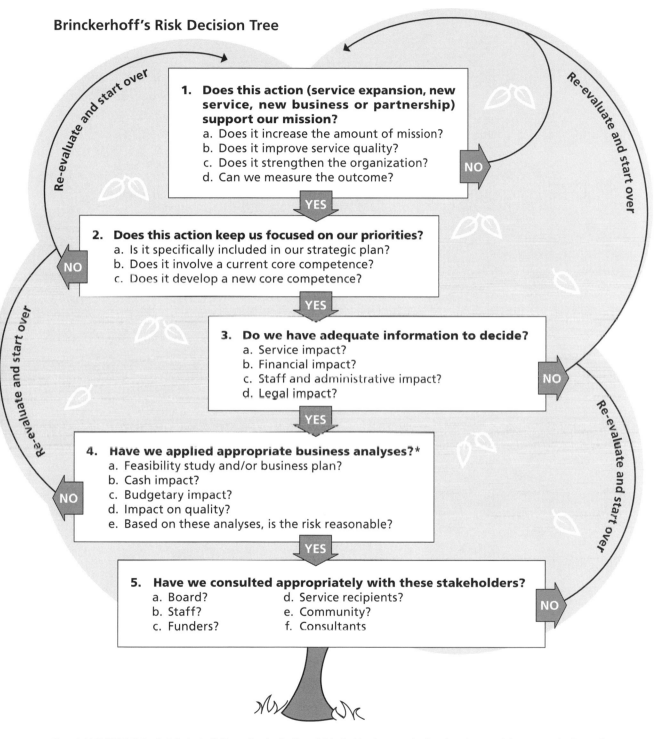

1. **Does this action (service expansion, new service, new business or partnership) support our mission?**
   a. Does it increase the amount of mission?
   b. Does it improve service quality?
   c. Does it strengthen the organization?
   d. Can we measure the outcome?

2. **Does this action keep us focused on our priorities?**
   a. Is it specifically included in our strategic plan?
   b. Does it involve a current core competence?
   c. Does it develop a new core competence?

3. **Do we have adequate information to decide?**
   a. Service impact?
   b. Financial impact?
   c. Staff and administrative impact?
   d. Legal impact?

4. **Have we applied appropriate business analyses?***
   a. Feasibility study and/or business plan?
   b. Cash impact?
   c. Budgetary impact?
   d. Impact on quality?
   e. Based on these analyses, is the risk reasonable?

5. **Have we consulted appropriately with these stakeholders?**
   a. Board?   d. Service recipients?
   b. Staff?   e. Community?
   c. Funders?   f. Consultants

Re-evaluate and start over

Using a Business Plan to Reduce Risk

Pretty much everyone has heard stories of entrepreneurs who come up with the idea for their zillion-dollar company on the back of a cocktail napkin. Well, the idea may have shown up over drinks, but the business plan sure didn't. Business plans are hard work, but they are not an unknown quantity. The how-tos are widely available. You can go to a day-long class on business planning, or you can earn an MBA. You can go to a number of web sites for step-by-step instructions, or you can use one of half a dozen good software packages.

Let's look at the purpose of the business planning process from the perspective of a steward:

> *Business planning is designed to reduce the risk of significant actions to a reasonable level, and to avoid actions whose risk is higher than the organization wishes to bear at the current time. It does this best when the information contained in the plan is complete, easily understood, and presented objectively.*

Remember, the board is *investing* some of the resources of the organization in this action. Unfortunately, many business plans are not written objectively. Often they are written to convince the board or staff or executive director that this business idea is the best thing since the invention of the Chia Pet. They underestimate potential problems, overestimate positive cash flow, and downplay negative market research (or don't even bother with it). The result of plans like this is, of course, to *increase* the risk to the organization, rather than decrease it.

The process outlined on the next page, in combination with information from the Resources section and outside help as needed, will help you get a good plan in place. Let's start with the process and then look at the biggest problems people have in the business planning effort.

Business planning for not-for-profit organizations

There are seven steps in the steward's not-for-profit business plan:

1. Review your mission statement.
2. Assess your willingness to take risk.
3. Decide on the motivational mission outcomes of your business and your profits.
4. Generate business ideas.
5. Develop feasibility studies.
6. Develop a full business plan.
7. Implement the plan.

Steps 4 through 7 are standard business practices. The first three steps, though, are designed to meet the unique needs of not-for-profit organizations as they enter the business planning cycle. These three steps ensure that mission outcomes stay the highest priority and that people throughout the entire organization, not just the executive or the board, are informed and enthusiastic about the process. *Do not* skip these three steps, as they ensure that the requisite support, direction, or focus on mission are in place (or not—in which case the project should be abandoned).

1. Review your mission statement

At the beginning of any large undertaking such as a business plan, it is always wise to review your plan with your business planning team (see the next paragraph), and to talk through the limitations of the mission. These limitations may be geographic (XYZ agency serves the Cook County population by...) or demographic (XYZ agency serves youth by...) or some combination of both. It is wise to review these now, as business that is done outside those limitations will require different reporting, different accounting, and may be considered unrelated business income and thus incur taxation if you make a profit. Go over your mission first.

Now, you can't—and more importantly, *shouldn't*—do this work in a vacuum. Establish an entrepreneurial team (name it whatever you want) made up of a couple of business-minded board members, someone from each level of the organization vertically (each level of management from top down to line staff) and each area of the organization (think each major part of your organizational chart). This group should establish your mission goals and oversee the planning. Depending on the type and scale of the potential risk, you may also want to include some key stakeholders from outside the organization.

2. Assess your willingness to take risk

Reasonable risk is good stewardship, but the definition of "reasonable" is not universally agreed on. Everyone on your board and everyone on your staff has a different internal risk quotient. Since entrepreneurial activities are by definition risky, you need to assess the group's willingness to take risk with your organization's assets *now*, not later. Better to do this before the board decides that X thousand dollars is too much to risk.

There are three resources at risk that you want to discuss: money, reputation, and morale.

Money is at risk both in the form of cash and in the form of people. The business will require you to invest cash and use your staff in new ways, or to hire new staff. *Reputation*, both for the organization and the individuals within it, is at risk. If the venture does not succeed, donors, corporate supporters, referral sources, and other stakeholders may lose faith in the organization. *Morale* is the third risk. New business cycles that include try (oops), try (oops), and try again (we did it!) are very common. Unless you explain the downside early, early "failures" could hinder staff morale.

During Step 2, everyone involved in the planning, as well as the full board, should discuss the risks inherent in the new idea, service, or business. The organization—especially the board—needs to develop risk limits for all money, reputation, and morale.

3. Decide on the *motivational* mission outcomes

This critical step is, unfortunately, the one most often botched. Establishing the mission outcome of your business idea and having that mission outcome be *motivational* is crucial at this stage. Why? New projects require board and staff to do more work, take more risk, work more hours—and they can distract from other mission tasks.

Thus the need for you to establish a mission outcome *that motivates your board and staff* to do all the work a business planning process requires.

FOR EXAMPLE: An organization that provides services to adults with disabilities wants to start a business that employs these people in competitive jobs, integrated with people without disabilities. As the staff begins looking at various business ideas, the executive staff sets some mission outcome goals for the business and for its profits. These are as follows:

1. Employ six people with disabilities in the first year, and twelve by the end of the third year of the project.

2. Use one-third of the profits of the business to fund recreational trips for other people with disabilities who are currently unfunded by the state and federal governments.

3. Use one-third of the profits of the business to reroof the administration building.

Note: the final third of the profits are to be reinvested in the business to help it grow.

The first two goals are highly motivational. The first speaks to what the business will do to help the core service group of the organization through its business activities; the second earmarks some of the profits for a mission-appropriate use. (The third also addresses what will happen to some of the profits, but how excited do *you* get about roofing issues? Me neither.)

To be motivational, outcomes should provide a short, straight line between the new work and the people you serve. Do all profits have to go directly to people? No. Some of it should go into reserves, or reinvested into the business, or even into roofing. But a meaningful amount should go to visible, tangible, *motivating* mission.

4. Generate business ideas

This step is important whether you already have a business idea, or are searching for one, or feel that you want a service idea, not a business idea. Using a facilitator, your entrepreneurial team should meet with groups of staff (no more than thirty at a time) with the following agenda: 1) review the mission goals for the new venture; 2) generate ideas for other ventures the organization could undertake. The facilitator should run this as a brainstorming session; all ideas are treated politely and there is no criticism. The session should generate venture ideas that either directly achieve the mission or make enough money to support the mission, that are based on a core competency, and that reflect a demand in the community that the organization serves. Then, after the session, the entrepreneurial team can sift through the ideas and pick the best two or three to pursue in the feasibility stage.

This method increases ownership among staff, adds a level of understanding about any new venture that surfaces, and, most importantly, tells staff loud and clear that you want to hear about new ideas in the future.

Note: Even if you already have a promising idea in mind, follow this step, facilitator, brainstorming, and all. You'll engage your staff and may well come up with some other great ideas, even ones better than yours! Be open and listen.

5. Develop feasibility studies

Feasibility studies come in two sizes: preliminary and final. The preliminary feasibility study is used to winnow the two or three ideas you have selected down to a final idea for in-depth analysis.

Preliminary feasibility studies are quick. They should take no more than two or three days, and they can be summarized in two or three pages. They should do the following in a preliminary manner.

- Define:
    - The product or service
    - The markets
    - The markets' needs and wants

- Measure the markets: Who are they? Are they stable, growing, or shrinking?
- Explore the industry: Is it expanding? How competitive is it? Is it moving offshore? and so forth

In doing these preliminary studies, you'll see which ideas fit best with your capabilities. For example, some ideas may take more time, more money, or more expertise than you have. Others may not fit with your mission, or with the way you provide mission. But one idea may well stand out. If so, take it and proceed to the final feasibility study.

Final feasibility studies are longer and more involved, and when you are through, you've done most of the heavy lifting associated with the development of the business plan. The work may take a few weeks or even a few months, and when you are done, you should have a feasibility study that covers the following areas:

- Introduction
- Market/product/service information
- Assumptions
- Start-up costs
- Financials
- Discussion of feasibility

A surprising number of feasibility studies don't really discuss feasibility. In fact, the entire idea is to do just that—to decide if the idea is feasible in the current environment. So make sure your opinion is in there.

Because of all the work everyone has put in, there is often a huge temptation at this point to adopt the idea whether or not it is *really* feasible. Listen to your numbers, and move from preliminary feasibility to final, and from final feasibility to the business plan, *only* if you are reasonably sure that the concept is—feasible. Remember, this is a risk reduction process, designed to weed out impractical or unrealistic (and thus high-risk) ideas. Use the process for that purpose, and move ahead only if your numbers and your market conditions make sense.

6. Develop a full business plan

Now you need to develop the entire plan, but only if the numbers are good. Most business plans follow something like the outline here.

I. Title page
II. Table of contents
III. Summary
IV. Description of your organization
V. Description of the market/service/product
VI. Marketing plan
VII. Financial plan
VIII. Business goals and objectives
IX. Appendices

You may well want to engage an outsider to help you put your plan together. If so, talk to your chamber of commerce, the business school at a nearby university, or your local United Way or Community Foundation for ideas and referrals.

A couple of hints on financials. Include at least the following financial displays in your plan.

- Sources and applications of funds: where your money is coming from and going to

- Balance sheets: showing your starting day and the end of years one and two

- Profit and loss statements: by month for the first year and by quarter for the next two years

- Break-even analysis

- Cash flow: by month for the first year and by quarter for the next two years

There are a variety of good business planning software packages on the market. These often force you to ask tough questions, and they will generate many of the financial displays for you.[7]

---

[7] For a free business development process, downloadable in PDF, go to www.missionbased.com, and follow the link for "Free Stuff." Or directly download it at http://www.missionbased.com/freestuff/adbusplancourse.pdfunder

7. Implement the plan

Once the researching, interviewing, and writing are done, you have to make the business happen—not only launch it, but make midcourse corrections. As you contemplate adjustments, keep your mission and your goals for the business closely at hand. It's easy to get distracted and forget your way.

Now that you know the business planning process, let's see if we can focus on error avoidance.

Avoiding errors in not-for-profit business plans[8]

Business plans help reduce risk, but there are some common mistakes made when using the plan. Here they are, in ascending order of importance and prevalence:

10. People don't read the projections after they are prepared.

 9. The financials don't support the goals of the business.

 8. The numbers and text don't jibe.

 7. No cash flow projection—or only an annual one.

 6. Inadequate estimate of days receivable.

 5. People don't understand break even analysis.

 4. People forget Murphy's Law.

 3. Inadequate cash reserves.

 2. Prices set too low.

 1. The plan did not include all of the costs.

Let's look at each in detail.

---

[8] I created this list of common errors as I helped not-for-profits nationwide develop their business ideas. I assumed that these were unique to the not-for-profit community. Then I met with some business-school types who told me that in their consulting with Fortune 500 companies, they see all these mistakes! So apparently these are universal business plan errors. Isn't it heartening to know we're not alone in our mistakes?

10. People don't read the projections

The staff and entrepreneurial committee spend days, weeks, *months* preparing a business plan full of great information, and the board merely skims it. Is it just that the board trusts the committee? Perhaps. Or is the plan so large, so imposing, or *so poorly written* that no one but the hardest-core business plan addict would even crack the cover? Sometimes. Regardless of the reason, the result is consistent. Ten weeks or ten months or two years after adopting the venture plan you hear a complaint from the board: "I didn't realize we were investing *that* much money!"

Solution: Three strategies can help solve this problem. First, be brief in your writing and put background material in the appendices. Second, have an executive summary. This should be written last, but it should appear first, and include only key information such as a description of your service, the markets, and financial summaries. Executive summaries should rarely exceed five pages. Third, when the plan is brought before the board for action, hold a thorough discussion of not only the plan itself but its implications as well, emphasizing the fact that there is no sure thing. Make sure your board members have been told the mission outcomes and the mission risks.

9. The financials don't support the goals of the business

Surprisingly, many plans include financial statements that show the plan is doomed to fail. To avoid this, maintain focus and consistency through multiple revisions of the planning process.

> FOR EXAMPLE: A performing arts organization I worked with wanted to do more performances in elementary schools to expose more children to classical music. There was no money in the budget, so they were seeking entrepreneurial ventures to fund these youth concerts. About four months after I met with them to discuss their mission goals (the in-school youth concerts), I got a call from the director. She was excited about a contract with a local school district that would use the symphony's musicians to provide master classes in high schools. She asked if I would review their plan, and I agreed. As I examined the document, I noted that the youth-concert goals

were properly and prominently featured in the plan's introduction and rationale. But it was clear that these mission goals were not going to be realized.

The goal failure was built right into the plan. Even the most optimistic projections for the teaching contract only foresaw a total profit of just 12 percent of what they needed to fund one concert, let alone the five concerts that were their actual, stated goal. Each concert would cost $1,000 but the teaching contract profits were only projected at $120. How were they expecting to pay for five concerts (at a total cost of $5,000) with just $120 in net income from teaching? When I called the director and pointed this out, she said quietly, "Oh, yes. Well." And there was a long silence. I waited. "I suppose our goals have changed." I suggested that they might then want to change the wording of the business plan to lower expectations.

Solution: There are two lessons here. First, stick to your goal—or make a conscious decision to change it. Here the symphony got distracted from its goal, resulting in an interesting program, but one that was not financially sustainable. Second, invite a skeptical (or at least objective) person outside the entrepreneurial team to examine the plan for inconsistencies.

8. The numbers and text don't jibe

FOR EXAMPLE: A plan's text calls for $200,000 in debt to finance receivables, describing a five-year loan at 6.5 percent. But the income and expense statements have no interest line item, and the cash flow projections show debt service on a loan of $50,000, not $200,000.

FOR EXAMPLE: The plan's text says that the business will provide 400 units of service in the second year. But the staffing projected in the financials allows for a maximum of 300 units of service (at full capacity, no sick days, no personnel vacancies).

Solution: Hire an outsider to scour the plan for inconsistencies. Get someone from a bank, your chamber of commerce, a business planning consultant (not one that helped you write the plan), a business professor at a local college or university, or a volunteer from the Senior Corps of

Retired Executives to thoroughly read the plan. Ask them to make sure your numbers and your text agree.

7. No cash flow projection—or only an annual one

As said earlier, cash is like oxygen. You run out, you die, and very soon. Without a cash flow projection, no one should fund you, and no one should approve your plan.

Project monthly for the first twelve months and quarterly for the next twenty-four months. An annual cash flow projection isn't sufficient. You have to prepare for your lowest cash-on-hand status, not just the general pattern in a calendar year.

6. Inadequate estimate of days receivable

This issue can really sneak up and bite you. "Days receivable" is a realistic estimate of the length of time money is owed to you before it is paid. You have to prepare for this by having enough working capital. But people regularly underestimate days receivable and run out of cash. So let's look at the key reasons.

First reason: a customer misleads you. They promise to pay in 30 days and they have no intention of paying for 60, even 90 days.

Solution: Use caution, and check references for large customers.

Second reason: unclear definition of days until payment. Some customers calculate their payables from the day they post them, not the day you bill them. So 45 days can stretch to 60, even 75 pretty easily.

Solution: Make sure you ask your customers how quickly they pay, and *measure from what date*.

Third reason: slow billing. Most businesses bill weekly, even daily. Most not-for-profits bill monthly.

Solution: Figure out how often you can invoice and do it online if possible. Billing by e-mail saves money and gets the bill into the system faster; some accounts will even pay by direct deposit.

You need to get paid but just as importantly you need to know when you'll get paid. Be conservative here; money usually comes in later than expected.

5. People don't understand break-even analysis

Break-even analysis is a business projection that tells you the volume of product or service needed to cover all your costs this week, or this month, or this year. It is, at its heart, a volume number, and it is time sensitive. It is *not* an estimate of when the business will start making money.

> **FOR EXAMPLE:** Your widget factory costs $100,000 to run each year. Those costs (called *fixed costs*) are there even when no widget is produced. Each widget costs $2 in direct costs to make—labor, raw materials, waste, packaging—and sells for $3. The break-even point is the point at which direct costs and fixed costs balance out against the revenue the widgets generated. Take the price ($3) and subtract the direct costs ($2), resulting in a $1 contribution to fixed costs per widget. Divide that contribution into the total fixed costs ($100,000 divided by $1) and you will see that you must make and sell 100,000 widgets at *this price and cost level* to recover all costs *this year*.
>
> If the price could rise to $4 while costs stay the same, you could break even with 50,000 widgets. But if there is competition and you need to lower the price to $2.50, you have to sell 200,000 widgets and, darn it, the factory can only make 150,000 per year. That's a problem!

As you can see, breakeven is a really useful number. But it's *not* a projection of profit. I see organization after organization telling its board that, when they hit the 100,000-widget mark, the business will make money. Well, what about the two years before that 100,000-widget year, when you were losing your shirt, shoes, and hat?

The issue here is that staff will unwittingly promise things to their board that are untrue. And mistakes like that have a habit of coming around and punishing you later.

Solution: Be sure to explain to staff and board that breakeven means breakeven, not profit.

4. People forget Murphy's Law

We all know Murphy's Law: *Anything that can go wrong, will go wrong, and at the worst possible moment.* We all know that Murphy not only lives, Murphy *rules.* Then why do we assume that Murphy won't visit our business? He will, no matter how thorough our research and how masterful our projections.

Solution: Savvy businesses (for-profit and not-for-profit) set aside *contingency funds* for unforeseen circumstances. I think of these funds as simply *"Murphy Money."* Make sure you have some in your cash fund. Things *won't* go as you plan. Be prepared for the unforeseen.

3. Inadequate cash reserves

This is a combination of item 7 (cash flow), item 6 (receivables), and item 4 (Murphy's Law). The result is they run out of cash—that is, oxygen. Starting without adequate cash reserves is a far too common business-killer, and it is preventable.

Solution: Plan well; look at cash flow, not just income and expense; have some Murphy money put aside; go after your receivables with a passion (but not a vengeance). And have a backup plan, in the form of a line of credit that can be tapped in dire circumstances, as carefully laid out by you and your board.

Cash sufficiency planning is a job for your outside consultants, your banker, your accountant, and anyone on your board or staff who knows their spreadsheets and their business planning. Get help here. Prevention is better than cure when it comes to keeping your oxygen—your cash—flowing.

2. Prices set too low

Price is *never* about cost. Many if not most not-for-profits price their services (when they can set their prices) far too low. Many not-for-profits feel guilty about asking for *more* than their costs. But this simply sets the business up for failure. If you are diving into a new area, you are in a good position to set (or at least negotiate) your price, so listen up: Price is *never* about cost. It is always about *value*. If price was just about cost, we wouldn't have all those BMWs coolly clogging our streets, nor all those full first-class seats on airliners. Ritz would describe only a cracker, not a hotel chain, and Land's End would be a location, not a label. Get my point? If you add value, you can—and you *should*—increase price. Value can be hard things, like a guarantee, or soft things like empathy, understanding, or hours of operation. But people *do* value what you do. Never assume that the only way to appeal to them is by low cost. Don't sell yourself, your staff, or your mission short. Set a price that expresses the value of your work.

> **FOR EXAMPLE:** Years ago I helped a group of volunteers who needed some cash for their upcoming Vacation Bible School session. They decided to sell T-shirts with the Vacation Bible School theme and logo to their students and supporter. They discovered that they could get the shirts made for $4 each, but recoiled in horror when I suggested they sell them at $10 or even $20. "That's wrong!" one woman scolded. "Why is it wrong?" I answered. "Parents would be delighted to pay $10 for the shirt, knowing that any profits you make will go back to this ministry. You don't charge for admission. People understand that you have to make money somewhere." Eventually the group came around—and even found that they could double the price and sell out their supply to friendly customers happy to see the profits supporting the ministry.

Solution: Get help when you set your price, and remember the twin stewardship returns of mission and money. If the business has very high mission value, you can (but not necessarily should) plan for a lower return on your financial investment than a business with less relevance to the mission. But, as a steward, if someone is willing to pay you well for your work, don't be embarrassed by it—use that money to fulfill your mission. Never be embarrassed by income if you have earned it.

Don't sell yourself, your staff, or your mission short. Set prices that express the value of your work.

1. The plan did not include all of the costs

At the end of the day, after all your work in developing your business idea, getting your board and staff with the risk-taking program, doing your projections, and writing your plan, you want the darn thing to work. And sometimes those pesky numbers just don't balance out. So the temptation is to pull out some of the costs, to make the numbers run. (As noted in Chapter 7, Financial Stewardship, this is a common strategy in not-for-profits, often brought on by funder requirements.) DON'T!!! Include *all* your costs. Then make a good decision—which could still include operating a business at a loss, because of its contribution to the mission. But you cannot make such a decision if you don't have the information available.

So there they are, the ten biggest mistakes of business planning. If you are going to be the best steward, don't let these show up in your plans. The simple steps listed above can help you avoid most if not all of them.

The Results of Good Risk Taking

A lot of good can come from risk taking. Stewardship and mission benefits abound. Let's look at a list of outcomes that I have seen accrue to not-for-profits that take the entrepreneurial path.

- **More mission.** By innovating ways to serve people, risk taking can result in accomplishing more of your mission—through new or better services, new geographic or demographic markets, or other developments. Which is—let's not forget—the point!

- **More income.** New services should result in more income, perhaps more ability to spread administrative costs, and related benefits. But the idea here is not to have more income and then have *even more* expenses. Breaking even is okay (again, depending on the mission return) but making money is much, much better.

- **Income diversification.** This is certainly a major goal of many not-for-profits' business plans. They feel they are too dependent on state, federal, or local governmental funds, or perhaps one or two foundation grants, and they want to develop their venture to help diversify their income sources. (Be sure, however, not to have more businesses than you can attend to.)

- **More innovation.** When you gain comfort taking risk, you will try more new things—and those that work will become standard. More innovation will follow. And mission quality will improve.

- **Increased flexibility.** Taking risks makes the organization stronger and more flexible. Flexibility is crucial in today's rapidly changing environment.

- **A focus on core competencies.** One of the most important benefits of learning the business planning process and applying it regularly is that you learn to focus on what you do best—your core competencies. This focus is a result of the calculation of risk: you are less likely to fail if you know what you are doing. Do what you do well, and do a lot of it.

- **Improved efficiency.** Organizations become more efficient and more effective when they take good risk. The risk calculations force them to attend more to what works and what stakeholders want—and that usually makes for greater efficiency. It's more efficient to deliver a service people want than one they're not interested in. Finally, they focus on their core competencies, walking away from things that they don't do well. All of this helps them become more efficient and effective in their use of the organization's resources—and that's good stewardship.

Recap

In this chapter you learned how to manage program risks in your not-for-profit. You saw that good stewards take calculated risks, and you learned some tools for making sure that the risks your organization takes are reasonable and well understood.

We examined the social entrepreneur's decision process, which is similar to the stewardship decision-making model presented in Chapter 2—in fact, the only real difference is that the social entrepreneur is concerned specifically with risk analysis. Remember:

A *social entrepreneur* takes risk on behalf of the people his or her organization serves.

The business plan is the key tool in risk reduction. *Business planning* is designed to reduce the risk of significant actions to a reasonable level, and to avoid actions whose risk is higher than the organization wishes to bear at the current time. It does this best when the information contained in the plan is complete, easily understood, and presented objectively.

A feasibility study is the part of a business plan that examines an idea thoroughly, teasing out the potential problems (risks) and opportunities (rewards), and then laying out the entire issue so that a management team can decide whether the idea has merit and whether the risk is reasonable given the current circumstances.

The business planning process for not-for-profits includes:

1. Review your mission statement
2. Assess your willingness to take risk
3. Decide on the motivational mission outcomes
4. Generate business ideas
5. Develop feasibility studies
6. Develop a full business plan
7. Implement the plan

Diligent business planning doesn't eliminate problems—but some common mistakes are avoidable. These include:

1. People don't read the projections after they are prepared.
2. The financials don't support the goals of the business.
3. The numbers and text don't jibe.
4. No cash flow projections—or only an annual one.

5. Inadequate estimate of days receivable.

6. People don't understand the break-even analysis.

7. People forget Murphy's Law.

8. Inadequate cash reserves.

9. Prices set too low.

10. The plan did not include all of the costs.

Finally, we recalled the real reason you take risk: more mission outcome, in the form of seven potential benefits:

• More mission

• More income

• Increased flexibility

• Income diversification

• More innovation

• A focus on core competencies

• Improved efficiency

Taking risk is part of good stewardship. Balancing the tendency toward risk avoidance against the sometimes equal urge to take too many risks—that is the art of stewardship. Trying new services, or expanding rapidly, or getting into an unknown area just because funding is available: these can all pose risks beyond their benefit. Sometimes this is called "chasing the money," and it is often a recipe for disaster.

Take your risks, but take them prudently and knowledgeably, using the tools you have been shown here. Remember, the risks you are taking are not for your benefit, and they are not being taken with *your stuff*. Be a steward.

CHAPTER EIGHT DISCUSSION QUESTIONS

1. Do we take risks? What kind? If we don't succeed, do we act as though we've failed?

2. What kind of risks should we avoid? Why? Is increased risk-taking for our organization good stewardship or foolish?

3. Do we have adequate business planning skills on the staff or available in the community? Do we need to develop more staff skills in this area?

4. How do we foster innovation in our staff, and the acceptance of innovation and experimentation in our board?

5. Do we model for our staff a willingness to take risks and innovate? How can we improve at this?

CHAPTER NINE | Stewardship in Good Times and Bad

Growth is good, right? Well, mostly. Good stewards seek balance, especially the balance between needs in your community and resources to provide for those needs. Thus, while growth in services without a similar growth in revenue may mean increased efficiency, it may also mean that your service provision increase is moving faster than you can pay for it.

That's problem number one with growth: not enough money. Growth is the first topic in this chapter. Next we'll examine what you should do in a downturn, when times are bad and the organization must contract. There are some strategic and tactical issues to address, and we'll look at them in some detail. We'll also look at being a good steward during a crisis—and how a good steward takes care of himself or herself in a crisis.

Finally, we'll examine the all-important issue of staying focused in tumultuous times. It is so very easy to get distracted when the organization is growing—to get swept up in the exhilaration of the moment. Suddenly, you are no longer the mission-based organization you were before, and that may well not be a good thing. The same is true in a crisis. It is not uncommon for people to have knee-jerk reactions to financial or other kinds of crises, and as a result they may do more damage than the crisis presented initially. We'll learn how to keep our eyes on the prize, to paraphrase Dr. King.

By the end of this chapter, you will have a better understanding of how to deal with the big ups and downs that show up every so often like an unexpected guest at your door. You'll also have some checklists to refer to when the inevitable crisis (good or bad) does arrive.

Perhaps you have taken some kind of "life stress" test. You answer questions about key events in your recent life (usually twelve to eighteen months), and then add up your scores to get your stress level. But note that not all these events are "bad." In fact many, such as your wedding, the birth of a child, or a promotion, are considered life highlights, and thus don't pop into your mind as stressful, since we normally associate bad things with stress.

These tests show us that many good things are stressful too. That's worth remembering, for ourselves, our staff, our board, and our organization, as we examine the times when things go insanely well or terribly badly.

Stewardship during Growth

The more your organization grows, the more mission it can do, right? Perhaps.

The more your organization grows, the more money it'll have to do mission, correct? Maybe.

But growth is important, isn't it? Yes, usually.

Those three sets of questions and answers set the stage for us to talk about growth. Nearly everyone agrees that growth in organizations is a good thing: intuitively it suggests that we'll help more people and accomplish more mission. Certainly we want our mission statement to be realized as widely as possible, helping as many of our target recipients as we can.

But growth for growth's sake is not a good thing, and not good stewardship. If you grow too quickly, or too haphazardly, you can quickly do
one, two, or all three of these:

- Outrun your cash—go broke.

- Overtax your infrastructure—stress the systems to the breaking point.

- Reduce quality of services—dissatisfy everyone.

None of these is desirable, so let's look at each in a bit more detail. These
are things that you really don't want to have happen.

Outrun your cash

Over the years, I have seen at least fifty execs—good, solid managers
all—listen to the following example and say, "*Now* I understand why we're
always short of cash, even though we're growing in budget and not losing
money." If your organization is growing and short of cash, pay attention.

> FOR EXAMPLE: A foundation provides you with a million-dollar
> one-year grant for a service that you already do well, and that is a
> high priority in your strategic plan. You are told that the funder will
> pay all your expenses (direct and indirect) associated with the work,
> and you figure, "What do we have to lose? All our costs are covered,
> it's something we do well, and it's a priority…let's do it!"

Fine, but here's the bottom line. The funder pays you 45 days after
you bill them, and you bill them at the end of the first month of
work. That means 75 days of work before you get paid. If you take
the amount of the grant ($1 million) and divide it by 365 days in
the year, and multiply that by 75 (the number of days before you
get paid), whoops, that's $205,479. You have spent that much of
your money just to get the grant. Ouch. And that's real money, not
depreciation or some other accrual accounting mumbo jumbo. In
essence, you have provided your funder with a no-interest $205,479
loan for a year.

The $205,479 in the example is called "working capital," and it's the money you need to do your work between the time you do it and the time you get paid. And in the real world it would be even more because you would have start-up costs that would add to your early cash burden under the grant.

When you grow, you soak up cash. Where is the cash coming from? In this case, it would have to come from *prior years' earnings*. Organizations that have larger and larger income every year, yet only budget to break even, fall further and further behind this working capital curve, unless their funders pay them in advance—a rarity.

This is a huge problem. It is caused in part by funders, who continue to be unaware of how the procedure contributes to this problem, and in part by not-for-profit organizations' own naiveté about finance. You are no longer naive, so now you have to think about the cash cost of growth.

If you grow quickly, you need lots of cash. Where will it come from? Not from profits, if you only budget to break even. Be a good steward: plan for profit so that you can grow your mission when opportunities arise in the future.

Overtax your infrastructure

Most not-for-profits already have a shaky infrastructure. They do without a human services person, a marketing person, a technology specialist. They use old accounting software running on old computers with dial-up Internet connections. Their outcome measurement systems may be manual, and their filing is behind because they are short of office staff since the last budget cutback, so they can't find documentation they need. Their funders fuss about administrative percentage of budget, so they scrimp there, and all the admin staff have far, far too much to get done in one lifetime already.

Sound familiar? Sadly, it is far, far too familiar. Not to suggest that you spend more on your infrastructure right now, but it probably merits some review in your next planning and budgeting discussion. Since the year

The Cost of Growth

Growth is exciting, but it can be expensive! Every year, for every program, look at the difference in size of the program in terms of funds, and the number of days it takes to get paid. If you assume the program is breaking even, or if it is budgeted to break even, you can calculate your cash loss from program growth by using the following formula:

(difference in program income ÷ 365 days)

X

(number of days until funder pays)

For example, your day program's income will rise from $115,000 this year to $127,000 next year. This program is paid for by your county Department of Services, which pays you in 50 days.

How much cash will this cost you? To find out, first subtract your next year's income from your current year's income to get your growth: $127,000–$115,000 = $12,000.

Then divide that by 365 days in the year: $12,000/365 = $32.87. Finally, multiply $32.87 by the number of days until payment (50): $32.97 x 50 = $1,643.83. What does that mean? It means that if your program grows by $12,000 next year, *and* it takes 50 days for you to get paid, *and* the program breaks even, your organization will be $1,643.83 poorer *in cash* at the end of the year than it is today.

If you do this for every program, you'll have a better idea of your cash impact when you do your budget. Remember, if you have a program that is shrinking, you'll wind up with lower working capital needs, and thus positive cash flow for that program. Finally, keep in mind that this example works when the program breaks even. If it loses money, things are worse; if it makes money, things will be better by *year end*, but not initially.

2000, foundations and corporations have been excited about funding "capacity building," even as critics in the press, or on oversight web sites such as Guidestar.com, harass the sector about having administrative costs that are too high. Foundations in many parts of the country have begun to fund nondirect costs, trying to build a stronger sector. That's a good trend, but not one that solves problems in rapid growth.

But for the purposes of our discussion here, the warning is that you can overtax an administrative structure just as surely as you can overload a car, or a train, or an airplane, with disastrous results.

> **FOR EXAMPLE:** A human services organization in the Southwest had expanded under a grant into a new form of family counseling to prevent divorce and child abuse. The method of counseling was new, and the counseling staff, while embracing the concept, had to be retrained in the new methodology. Outcomes needed to be measured in a more detailed way than anyone on the staff had ever done before. More staff had to be hired to handle the counseling load. More staff meetings had to be held to keep track of everything.
>
> All this work was done, done well, and done with surprisingly little problem—*but*…about ninety days into the grant, the executive discovered that the accounting system couldn't accommodate the demands of the grant. This created an expensive new problem for the organization, which hadn't considered the impact on accounting when applying for the innovative, mission-laden grant.

Remember that some overtaxation is obvious, as in the example above. Some is creeping: it shows up in missed deadlines, decaying quality, and stressed-out staff. Growth plans need to account for the staff and systems at the line of service *as well as* the people, equipment, and buildings that back them up.

Reduce quality of services

Impaired service quality is a problem in and of itself, as well as a result of the problems we just looked at: outrunning cash and outgrowing infrastructure. If the focus on the organization is solely on getting bigger, and particularly if the quality of services has always been good, it is easy for a manager to pay more attention to growth than to maintaining quality, since quality has been on "set and forget" for so long.

The decision model first introduced in Chapter 2 included two decision points regarding quality. There was a question about whether the decision could *improve* quality, and one regarding the *quality impact* of the decision.

The best way to attend to quality during expansion is to set up a system of quality metrics that allows you to look at trends. Here are some typical metrics used by various organizations: What are the trends in customer satisfaction before and after our growth? Staff turnover? Staff satisfaction? If the organization is accredited by an outside body, is it still meeting all of its accreditation criteria? Are new customers, consumers, or patrons still coming into the organization? How do customer evaluations after growth compare to evaluations before growth?

These factors can be measured by survey, but some focus groups—particularly of patrons—can help ensure that patrons are satisfied and that quality has not dropped.

Growth usually means helping more people, which is certainly a desirable stewardship outcome. It means challenging staff and board to do better, which is also good. But like any change, growth brings opportunity and potential adversity, so you need to approach growth wisely, with open eyes, making sure your core services do not suffer.

Stewardship during Contraction

Talking about growth is fun, even with the downsides described above. But talking about contraction—about reducing services—can't be good, can it? Actually, it can. But certainly when we have to contemplate cutting our budgets, and thus our services, a positive impact is not top-of-mind. This section provides some checklists of things to do and questions to ask when times suddenly get very bad.

FOR EXAMPLE: Your key funder calls you three months before the end of the fiscal year. Their message: The grant that makes up 40 percent of your overall income and 100 percent of any net you may retain has been cut by 30 percent as of the beginning of the fiscal year, and worse, you have to cut 10 percent from the remaining three months of this year's grant. If you thought life was stress-filled before, welcome to hypertension land.

In situations like this, we need to start by asking a few key questions.

- *How bad is the shortfall, really?* Is the news from our funder fact, or is it rumor based on rumor? Is it real and, if not, when will we know the real number? Is there any room for negotiation?

How to Use a Crisis Management Team

In times of crisis, assemble a crisis management team. This team should be made up of board, staff, your banker, your auditor, and perhaps even a representative of the people you serve. Use them for strategizing and figuring out your reaction to your cutback. This team should address the questions listed in this section. It should also run cash flow projections and create best-case, medium-case, and worst-case scenarios.

In doing your projections, you need to develop some decision points based on future events or future cash balances. After you run your weekly cash flow analysis and generate your scenarios, have your crisis team establish some *decision points*.

These are points in the scenarios that will result in a decision. For example, *If contract X is not renewed, we lay off three staff members and shut down these two services the next week*. You may have a number of such decision points, but having them in writing with your team will help structure your decision process.

Note: *Don't* share these points with all your staff unless you really, really want to panic people. These decision points have not yet arrived, so you don't *know* you are going to lay people off or shut down programs. You *may or may not* do it. Once you announce your decision points to your wider community, they will become cast in stone in many minds.

- *What is the cause of the shortfall?* Is the shortfall (as in the example above) a result of one funder's change of priority, or is this a wider, systemic issue such as an economic downturn?

- *Is the shortfall long-term or short-term?* Will we get through this in one fiscal year, or is this our new reality?

- *Are individual services at risk?* Are the cuts deep enough so that we can't do a particular service or set of services well and may have to cut them completely?

- *Is the organization's viability at risk?* Is the cutback deep enough and important enough that the organization might not survive? (The example above results in the loss of any profits.) Conversely, if the services being cut are central to the image of the organization, or the flow of services in the organization, its viability might also be at risk.

- *Are legal responsibilities or contractual obligations at risk?* In some cases, you can't just cut services pell-mell; you are required to keep services in place by contract. Review copies of all contracts and grant awards. Note unavoidable obligations and mark the potential controversies for a possible review by your attorney.

  FOR EXAMPLE: You have a transportation contract to provide routes in all parts of your community. You take a 20 percent hit in funder income and decide to cut four of your least-used routes. The problem? Those are the only four routes that serve a particular socioeconomic group in your community. You've just violated your contract.

Once you get through your starting questions, you need to look at a series of questions to focus your thoughts on both long-term and short-term reactions to the crisis. The most common response from managers is to deal with *tactical*, or short-term actions. This is a mistake. You need to first look at *strategic* or long-term actions. Taking the long view first is a better stewardship response. You can use a "stop, step back, and check the long view" process to help avoid knee-jerking responses that use up a lot of energy but don't really advance your cause.

FOR EXAMPLE: The best lesson about long view and short view comes from canoeists. If you've canoed, you know that when the water is calm, you can meander across the lake enjoying the scenery. When the wind and waves pick up, the only way to get to the far side is to pick a place on the far shore and focus on it. If you just watch the bow of the canoe (the short view) you'll go off course, and can even wind up going around in circles. You need to take the long view (the far shore) to accomplish your goal.

You need to start with the long view. The following two lists are actions you should consider and questions you should ask as you work your way through your crisis. Strategic first, then tactical.

Strategic tasks

- Review your mission and values statement—what does it say about priorities?
- Review your strategic plan—what does it say about priority services?
- Review your marketing plan—what markets are most important?
- Talk to peer organizations—are there appropriate group responses to the cuts?
- Talk to state trade associations—what are other organizations doing?
- Is there a need for long-term strategic restructuring such as merger or partnering?

Tactical tasks

- Run weekly cash flow projections—remember, cash is oxygen, and you are already in thin air.
- Inform staff and board early and often—but only tell them what you *know*, not what you *think may happen,* or what you are considering, or what might/could/should/ought to happen. The rumor curve is deadly.
- Review contractual obligations.
- Check state labor laws and union contracts for layoff and cutback limitations.

- Inform vendors of possible late bill payments.
- Inform creditors; this is simplified if your banker is on your crisis team.
- Develop best-case, middle-case, worst-case scenarios. Be conservative about all three.
- If layoffs are necessary, do them carefully, in complete accord with state regulations, union contracts, and best HR practices. Sooner is nearly always better with layoffs.
- Communicate, communicate, and communicate—with staff, volunteers, service recipients, community members, funders, vendors, and creditors.
- Prepare for media inquiry.

Making decisions

One of the toughest parts of crisis management is making crucial decisions. Do I lay these people off now, or wait? Do we cut back this program or that program? This is hard stuff, no doubt. But making a decision and being accountable for it is part of the job.

The biggest danger in decision making is delay. None of us likes making hard decisions, and we may wait as long as possible, optimistic that things may get better. We don't want to have knee-jerk reactions, but we do want to take care of our organization and our staff. And much as we want to get *all* the information before we decide, the reality is we can't get that information.

Good managers *always* want more information in hand before making a difficult, particularly a crucial, decision. In a crisis, there will always be another date approaching, another memo in the mail, another meeting coming up to help you delay decisions. Get used to the idea that you, as a leader, have to pick a point and *decide*.

Shrinking programs, staff, and mission is not fun. Good times and expansion years are almost always balanced out by some lean times. Ideally, "lean" will merely mean "not growing," and you will avoid the kind of drastic cutbacks discussed here.

But whether you are growing quickly, shrinking quickly, or staying even, you need to stay focused. That's the subject of our next section.

Staying Focused

Sometime in the late 1990s I was channel-surfing in a hotel room and saw a documentary on television's history. I didn't think I would really care much, but it was fun to see short bits of shows that I had grown up with, so I stayed with the program for a while. Then the subject changed to popular commercials from 1960 to 1985. I remembered all of the commercials well, but what struck me was how *boring* they seemed—they were *sixty whole seconds*! Some had shots that didn't cut away for ten or fifteen seconds. How dull. I switched to a network channel and closely watched the next two or three commercials, marveling in how many

---

Questions to Ask Yourself during Tumultuous Times

Whenever you face stressful times—good or bad—you've got to make an extra effort to be an effective steward and leader. Here's a list of stewardship questions for you to keep on your desk and review regularly as you work through your crisis.

- Am I getting adequate food, rest, exercise, and time with my family?

- Am I asking the hard questions?

- Do I have all the information I can get?

- Am I sharing information widely?

- If other staff have to take a financial cut, am I taking a bigger one?

- Am I leading optimistically?

- Am I putting mission first?

- Am I listening to everyone?

Regular attention to these questions can keep you focused and help you lead.

images, sounds, colors were crammed into ten or fifteen seconds. It was really sensory overload, but one that I had become de-sensitized to.

Our attention span has shortened, which makes it hard to stay on task for long. And lack of focus decreases efficient and effective use of resources. You can't be efficient or effective if you are changing course all the time. But how do we stay focused in good times and bad? How do we stay on course? The following four suggestions are drawn from previous material, but take on a special importance in the context of crisis management. They are:

- Focus on mission
- Focus on the strategic plan
- Focus on core competencies
- Focus on the business plan

Focus on mission

This should certainly not be a surprise to you by now. Start and end your discussions with mission. Post your mission statement on your computers' screensavers, put copies on your meeting tables at all meetings, read it aloud before meetings. As you make decisions, return over and over to your mission statement. Read the words aloud to yourself. Is this action, change, investment, or decision going to improve your mission-capability or mission-efficiency?

Focus on the strategic plan

Say you are driving in a part of town with which you are familiar, but not fluent, trying to make a meeting on time. You come upon an accident and must detour. You vaguely remember that there is a parallel route about a half-mile south, so you turn that way and promptly get lost. You're late, it's dark, it's raining, and now you're in a residential neighborhood, not exactly conducive to stopping and asking directions. Aren't you glad you have a map in your glove compartment?

The strategic plan is that map for your organization. When the unexpected occurs, it can help you get back on course. In other words, even if you aren't expecting a crisis, get your plan in order. Be sure to prioritize your services, your service markets (the people you help), and your funders. This not only allows you to focus on the most important things day to day and week to week, but also gives you guidance when a big opportunity for growth occurs, or when you are faced with difficult decisions in a cutback.

Focus on core competencies

Core competencies are what you consistently do well as an organization. If you do something well, do a *lot* of it. If you don't do something well, or don't know how to do it at all, don't take money from a funder for it. Don't take a grant that's going to lead you from your core competencies and cause a reduction in quality of service.

Stewards, figure out what you do well. If there is a competency you lack, invest in training, education, or a knowledgeable individual to bring your competency up to an acceptable level. Don't just accept any money from anybody for anything.

Note: Your core competencies should be listed in your business plan.

Focus on the business plan

As noted in Chapter 8, Taking Good Risk, business plans reduce risk by spelling out the funding and actions required to make your strategic plan succeed. The business plan contains your funding plan, and staying focused on that—especially things like cash flow and break-even analyses—will help you keep your house in order even as the tornado whirls around you. You may lose some shingles and siding, an outbuilding or two, but your foundation and structure will stay intact.

In good times and bad, it is so, so easy to get off track. There are many distractions and temptations facing you, your board, and your staff. Use the mission, your strategic plan, your core competencies, and your business plans and you'll do fine.

Recap

In this chapter, we discussed being a good steward when times are tumultuous. These can be good times, with rapid growth and more mission activities going out the door, or they can be heartbreaking times, with contractions of mission and people's needs going unmet. A steward is ready for both, and has the skills and the insights to get his or her organization through the change.

We started by looking into the issue of rapid growth, and how it is often far too seductive, resulting in one or more of three things happening. These three were:

• Outrun your cash—go broke.
• Overtax your infrastructure—stress the systems to the breaking point.
• Reduce quality of services—dissatisfy everyone.

We studied examples of each of these problems and how to avoid them.

Then we looked at financial and service contraction, and strategic as well as tactical issues during contraction. We also examined the key stewardship questions that need to be answered in a crisis.

Since both happy and sad change can bring on a loss of focus, we ended by discussing ways in which you, as a good steward, can keep your organization on track. These include focusing on mission, using your strategic plan, rallying around your core competencies, and applying your business planning skills.

Rapid growth or rapid contraction can arrive like a welcome guest—or a wild uncle—at the door. Now you know where to *start* when that unexpected guest arrives. They may drop in just for coffee, or may move their stuff into the guest room for a long stay. They may be a great addition to the household or a very, very disruptive force. In any of these situations, you need to be able to use your skills to keep your house and your family—your not-for-profit—well, safe, and continuing to function with your values and mission intact.

This chapter wraps up the suggestions, coaching, stories, and ideas on stewardship. It's time for you to go out and get started with your stewardship journey, and the next chapter will get you on the way. It's a pair of self-assessments: one for your organization, and one for you—plus some warning signs of trouble in the organization. So get going!

CHAPTER NINE DISCUSSION QUESTIONS

1. Are we focused on our long-term goals?

2. Do we consider these goals both when we grow and when we shrink?

3. Do we have our priorities set so that they can guide us in a crisis?

4. Should we be building a cash reserve to be ready to grow, or to help us if we have to shrink?

5. Do we need to update our media policies to prepare for media inquiry if our funder cuts services?

6. What are our core competencies? What are we really good at organizationally?

CHAPTER TEN

Taking Stock
of Stewardship

By now you should have a good idea of what it takes to be a steward. We've reviewed the characteristics of a mission-based steward, and we've looked at three specific roles—those of board, staff, and funders. I've given you quite a few examples and a number of hands-on ideas for applying the stewardship concepts.

Now it's time for you to do an initial self-assessment in three parts: an organizational "self-assessment," a personal self-assessment of your own actions and attitudes, and a scan for signs of organizational trouble.

By the end of this chapter you should have a good handle on where you are personally and organizationally. That will give you a starting spot, a benchmark from which to measure your progress as you move down the stewardship path.

A note about self-assessments: First and foremost, an assessment is not a one-time event. That is, you can't take the test, score yourself, and then forget about it. It's the first step in self-improvement. If you score well, great! But don't forget about trying to improve even more. If you score poorly, don't panic! You're just learning something every good steward wants to know: ways to make your organization better. This is just a starting place, not the finish line. Don't despair.

A suggestion about process: Don't do these self-assessments alone—particularly the organizational self-assessment. Copy the following pages and have all of your management team fill them out individually. Then do one of two things: have someone average all the scores and present the team with the results or, better yet, get together in a group and report out (and record) each person's results. Use this time as a jumping-off point for discussion, and to make a list of things that need to be worked on. If possible during that meeting, assign responsibility and deadlines and get going.

If you fill out the organizational stewardship assessment on your own, it will reflect too many of your own biases, good and bad, about the organization. Doing this as a group brings more objectivity and, beneficially, wider ownership to implement needed changes that surface through the assessment process. Work as a team. Include your key management staff and board officers to start. You may also want to include key outsiders or selected mid-management and line staff if appropriate.

But what about your personal stewardship self-assessment? Doing a personal self-assessment in a group is much less comfortable. After conducting the organizational stewardship assessment as a group, you or your group leader (perhaps the executive director or board president) should hand out the personal self-assessment to all participants, and have them complete it on their own. Tell them that the assessment is only for your personal reflection and improvement, but that you will talk about the results in an upcoming staff meeting. At that meeting, ask people what they learned and what they are going to work on, if they want to share that with the group. As a leader, of course, you need to start the discussion by opening up, confessing what you learned, and talking about what you are going to work on. This method puts the key stewardship concepts on the table, and will optimally be the beginning of regular interaction and coaching on the methods needed to improve individual as well as organizational stewardship.

An Organizational Stewardship Assessment

This self-assessment is based on the characteristics of successful not-for-profit organizations we reviewed in Chapter 2. These nine important characteristics are:

1. A viable mission

2. A businesslike board

3. A strong, well-educated staff

4. Technological savvy

5. Social entreprencurism

6. A bias for marketing

7. Financial empowerment

8. A compelling vision

9. Tight controls

Use of Stewardship Assessment Forms

The stewardship assessment forms in this book are the creation of Peter Brinckerhoff, copyright 2004, and published by Fieldstone Alliance. We encourage you to copy these forms and distribute them to your board, leadership team, and other stewards. Use them! However, please do not use them without the included copyright information; do not distribute them for commercial purposes or resale; and do not use them unless you or your organization has purchased a copy of this book. See the copyright page of this book to learn more about using this material.

To make this even easier, the assessment is also available online at the publisher's web site at the following URL.

http://www.FieldstoneAlliance.org/client/inventory_tools/stewardship_inventory.cfm

By following the simple instructions at the web site, you can fill out the assessment and your results will be tallied for you.

HANDS-ON

I originally developed a self-assessment tool based on these characteristics for *Mission-Based Management Workbook.*[9] In this one, however, the questions and the scores focus on stewardship.

As you move through the self-assessment, remember that scores can be positive or negative, and that the sum for each characteristic will be re-entered in the summary at the end. After you re-enter and total your scores, you can compare your results to the scale provided.

Remember, this is just an initial look. Don't despair if your score is far below the ideal total. This is part of measuring: you have to know where you are starting. Alternatively, if you reach a very high score, congratulate yourself, but don't relax. A wise man once said that the road to excellence never ends—you never get there.

Note that these criteria are designed for a wide audience; some may not pertain to your organization. Adjust the scores accordingly.

[9] Peter Brinckerhoff, *Mission-Based Management Workbook and CD-ROM* (New York: John Wiley & Sons, 2000).

Organizational Stewardship Assessment

Mission Stewardship	Yes	No
Has your mission statement been reviewed by your board and staff within the past two years?	2	-2
Does staff use the mission statement as an aid to decision making and management? Are copies on the table at every meeting?	3	-1
Is the current mission statement on file with the Internal Revenue Service?	2	0
Is the mission statement short and focused enough for staff and board to learn it and be able to quickly recite it?	2	-1
Does the board refer to the mission statement when considering adding or dropping services? Are copies on the table at every meeting?	3	-1
Is the mission statement among the criteria used in personnel evaluations?	3	0
Total of column score (Add each column up and put the answer here)		
TOTAL SCORE: MISSION (Add total scores from Yes and No columns and put the answer here)		

Board of Directors Stewardship	Yes	No
Does the board view expenses as investments in mission?	3	-3
Does the board get regular training on the organization's financials?	2	0
Does the board have a mandated policy of turnover? (Are there set terms for board members? A limit on the number of consecutive terms?)	2	-2
Does the board have a written list of its responsibilities?	3	-4
Is there a current, written board manual?	1	-1
Does the board annually evaluate the head staff person, in person and in writing?	3	-3
Is the board involved in strategic planning on a consistent and regular basis?	2	-1
Is time set aside at each board meeting for ongoing orientation about the organization's work?	2	-1
Does the board annually approve the budget and then monitor it on a regular basis?	3	-4
Total of column score (Add each column up and put the answer here)		
TOTAL SCORE: BOARD OF DIRECTORS (Add total scores from Yes and No columns and put the answer here)		

Staff Stewardship	Yes	No
Does the organization chart and culture place the people that the organization serves in the primary (top) position?	3	-1
Do supervisors consistently act in ways to support the people they supervise?	3	-2
Are staff from all parts of the organization and all levels of management asked to serve on most staff committees?	2	-1
Are staff evaluations done at least annually, in writing and in person?	3	-2
Is there an active continuing education program for all staff?	3	0
Are staff encouraged to innovate and take risks?	2	0
Do staff formally evaluate their supervisors?	2	-1
Do staff see the financials of the organization regularly?	3	-1
Is there a staff recognition program? Was it designed by staff (not management)?	1	-1
Total of column score (Add each column up and put the answer here)		
TOTAL SCORE: STAFF (Add total scores from Yes and No columns and put the answer here)		

Technology Stewardship	Yes	No
Does your board and staff consider technology an important investment in mission?	3	-1
Do you have a person or committee responsible for using technology in providing mission?	3	-2
Does the group regularly review organizational tech security?	3	-2
Does the organization do a quarterly (four times a year) technology assessment?	3	-1
Does the organization have a designated tech specialist?	1	-1
Do staff get access to training in software and hardware use?	3	-2
Do senior management attend this training as well as line staff?	3	-1
Does the organization subscribe to a periodical that covers not-for-profit technological issues?	1	0
Total of column score (Add each column up and put the answer here)		
TOTAL SCORE: TECHNOLOGY (Add total scores from Yes and No columns and put the answer here)		

Entrepreneurial Stewardship	Yes	No
Does your organization review the mission return and the financial return of every investment (and view expenditures as investments?)	3	0
Has the organization investigated (or are you now doing) nontraditional activities to supplement income?	3	0
Have you discussed with your board and staff the value of risk in service and how it fuels innovation?	2	-2
Do you reward innovation and risk in your staff evaluations?	2	0
Are core values and the mission statement discussed when major innovations are considered?	2	-1
Do you and your board seek to continuously improve services?	2	-2
Are your service improvement efforts tied to your marketing and asking activities?	2	-2
Total of column score (Add each column up and put the answer here)		
TOTAL SCORE: ENTREPRENEURIAL (Add total scores from Yes and No columns and put the answer here)		

Marketing Stewardship	Yes	No
Do you know precisely who your organizational markets are for funders, referral sources, and people you serve?	3	-3
Have all your staff had customer satisfaction training in the past year?	2	-1
Have you asked your target markets what they want, or how satisfied they are with your services in the past 24 months?	3	-1
Does your web site have much more detail and depth than your printed materials?	2	-1
Have your written materials been developed to focus on your target markets?	1	-1
Do you update the information on your web site at least every 30 days?	2	-2
Are you constantly trying to improve your services from your customers' point of view?	2	0
Do you regularly talk to your staff about the differences between needs and wants?	2	0
Total of column score (Add each column up and put the answer here)		
TOTAL SCORE: MARKETING (Add total scores from Yes and No columns and put the answer here)		

Financial Stewardship	Yes	No
Have you achieved your target level of cash on hand?	2	0
Has your organization been profitable over the last three years taken together?	3	-1
Do you have a financial stewardship team that includes your banker, accountant, and members of your board and staff?	2	-1
Do you know which of your programs make money and which lose money?	3	-1
Do you have an endowment?	2	0
Do you and your board view your expenditures as investments in mission?	2	0
In your budgeting, do you review the financial return on any investment?	2	-1
In your budgeting, do you review the mission return on any investment?	2	-1
Do you share your financial information widely inside the organization?	2	-2
Do you have a banker with whom you meet regularly?	1	0
Do you have an active fundraising function?	2	-2
Total of column score (Add each column up and put the answer here)		
TOTAL SCORE: FINANCIAL (Add total scores from Yes and No columns and put the answer here)		

Vision and Planning Stewardship	Yes	No
Do you look beyond your current fiscal year for your capital planning?	4	0
Do you have a 3- to 5-year marketing plan?	3	0
Do you have a 3- to 5-year strategic plan?	4	-2
Are both board and staff involved in the strategic planning process?	3	-2
Do you share your draft plans widely both inside and outside the organization?	3	-1
Does your planning process include in some manner the people you serve, the funding sources, and the community?	3	-3
Do you have a permanent long-range planning committee?	3	-1
Do you hold yourself accountable for the goals and objectives in the plan through regular review of progress?	3	-1
Total of column score (Add each column up and put the answer here)		
TOTAL SCORE: VISION AND PLANNING (Add total scores from Yes and No columns and put the answer here)		

Controls Stewardship	Yes	No
Do you have the following policies, and have they been updated within the past 24 months?		
Bylaws	3	-3
Conflict-of-interest policy	2	-2
Financial policies	2	-3
Personnel policies	2	-3
Media policies	2	-1
Quality Assurance policies	2	0
Disaster Preparedness policies	2	0
Volunteer policies	3	-2
Do you train board and staff in these policies annually as appropriate?	3	-2
Total of column score (Add each column up and put the answer here)		
TOTAL SCORE: CONTROLS (Add total scores from Yes and No columns and put the answer here)		

Organizational Stewardship Assessment Score Compilation

Transfer the score for each area, and then sum your total self-assessment score at the bottom of the form.

Area	Your Score	Possible High Score
Mission		15
Boards		21
Staff Management		22
Technology		20
Social Entrepreneurship		16
Marketing		17
Finance		23
Vision & Planning		26
Controls		21
Total Stewardship Self-Assessment Score		181

A Personal Stewardship Self-Assessment

Now that you know where your organization stands as a steward, it's time to look at your personal stewardship abilities. As with the overall organizational self-assessment, copy the following pages, fill in the scores, and calculate your total. Date it so you can revisit it in six months to a year.

A final encouragement: be hard on yourself, or at least seriously objective. No one but you will see this assessment; you shouldn't post it on your staff bulletin board or e-mail it to all your friends. This is for you and you alone, so be fair, but not easy on yourself. The idea is to improve.

The self-assessment covers the eight characteristics of a mission-based steward that we reviewed in Chapter 1. To refresh your memory on these, they were:

1. Balance
2. Humility
3. Accountability
4. Integrity
5. The ability to motivate
6. A thirst for innovation
7. Communication skills
8. A quest for lifelong learning

Read and answer the questions, considering the *truth* about yourself. It does no good delude yourself about this.

The following assessment doesn't provide a score, but rather a series of questions for reflection. This approach reduces the tendency to be either unrealistically hard or easy on ourselves. Use the questions as food for thought about ways to improve as a steward. (You'll notice that some questions show up in more than one area. This is intentional.)

Balance

- Am I willing to find resources before we start to provide a service?

- Do I emphasize mission over money? Money over mission?
- Do I try to keep the staff and board well balanced when it comes to mission and money?
- Do I balance my work and my family appropriately?
- Do I delegate enough? If not, why not?

Humility

- Do I say "please" and "thank you" to everyone, every time I ask for something?
- Which do I say more often when describing the organization and its services: "I / my" or "we / our"?
- Do I delegate enough, realizing that I can't be expert at everything?
- Am I willing to listen to someone younger, less experienced, less tenured?

Accountability

- Do I report my actions and decisions fully to my supervisor or the board?
- Do I take full and complete responsibility for my actions and the actions of any staff I supervise?
- Do I ever try to "pass the buck" to someone else?
- Am I willing to make decisions appropriate for my job description?

Integrity

- Do my actions reflect the values of the organization? How, specifically?
- Do I model innovation for my staff? Am I willing to change?
- Do I model lifelong learning for my staff? How?
- Do I play by the same rules as the rest of the staff (dress code, work time, attendance at all staff training)
- Do I take responsibility for my actions and those of the people I supervise?

The ability to motivate

- Am I willing to pitch in at any level of work to get a large job done or a significant crisis solved?
- Do I take responsibility for my actions and those of the people I supervise?
- Am I visible as a leader?
- Do I lead optimistically?
- Do my employees know that I will always back them up if they do what I ask them to?
- Do I challenge my employees supportively, helping them learn and grow?

A thirst for innovation

- Do I urge my staff to try new things and, when they do, do I commend them?
- Am I aware that experimentation does not always produce the desired results?
- Am I willing to try new things personally?
- Do I willingly contribute ideas to large discussions, or am I hesitant?
- Do I enjoy brainstorming, or is it painful?

Communication skills

- In conversations, do I listen, or do I just wait my turn to talk?
- Do I share information freely with staff and peers?
- Have I been to a public speaking course in the past five years to refresh my skills?
- Am I out and accessible to staff regularly so that they can talk to me?
- Am I supportive of internal transparency with my board and staff?
- Do I read all my written correspondence aloud (to ensure it makes sense) before I send it (memos, letters, e-mail)?

- Do I try to communicate in a variety of styles, to appeal to a wide range of people?

Quest for lifelong learning

- Have I read at least one management or business book pertinent to our organization in the past twelve months?

- Have I visited a peer organization in the past twelve months to learn what they are doing well?

- Have I attended all the mandatory training my staff attends?

- When I attend out-of-town meetings, do I bring back what I learned and share it with others?

- Have I learned a new skill of any kind in the past eighteen months? (For example: CPR, computer security, small-engine repair, gardening—anything!)

- Do I read my local newspaper and a weekly news magazine thoroughly and regularly?

Again, remember that this is a first look at your stewardship improvement baseline. You now know what is great, what is good, and what needs improvement in your personal quest to become a better steward. Knowing where you are, and what you need to work on, either to enhance already good behaviors, or to fix those habits in need of repair, is the first step in self-improvement. The very fact that you were willing to take a self-assessment is laudable. Even if you aren't thrilled with your answers, good for you for starting the process!

Signs of Trouble

You've completed the often-difficult task of looking inward—at your organization and yourself. But don't get caught navel-gazing while a storm brews! Following is a list of symptoms of organizations that are either in trouble, or about to be. Think of these as storm warnings. Some may just be dark clouds on the far horizon, a storm that may or may not come your way. However, some of these warning signs are comparable to the green sky that precedes a tornado.

The following signs are presented generally in order from the most urgent (and dangerous) to the least pressing. That being said, it does not mean that those items listed near the end are unimportant. If you see your organization here, particularly if you see more than two or three of these warning signs, start taking steps now.

No financial information being reported

Stewards who find that the financial information has stopped coming should run, not walk, to the organizational office and start pounding on the desk until the financials show up. Financial reporting is a crucial part of an organization's healthy checks and balances. There is no way that the board and staff can do their job as financial stewards without information, and the lack of that information nearly always means that something else, usually something very unpleasant, is going on. Is the organization out of money? Did someone blow through their budget limitations? Was debt taken on without board approval? Fraud? Conflict of interest? Waste? Any or all of these are possible, even likely.

Excessive staff turnover

If staff are coming and going right away, or if there seems to be a revolving door in the organization's employee ranks, there's a problem. It may be poor recruiting, it may be a rotten work environment (physically or culturally), it may be that the management team is all directly descended from Attila the Hun—but something is going on, and the board needs to find out what it is and ensure that it gets fixed. Heavy staff turnover is expensive in dollars (recruitment, training, orientation) and in mission (integrating new people takes existing staff away from their other work). Long-serving staff provide experience, consistency, and, usually, a sense of stability to the organization.

Note: The danger here is overreacting to the term "excessive," which is an extremely subjective word. I have served on the board of an organization in which one group of staff had an 80 percent annual turnover. When I inquired what the heck was going on, I learned that the national turnover norm for this kind of staff was 130 percent per year. Thus our turnover was "good."

Excessive board turnover—or lack of quorums

For the most part, this problem is the same as for staff. Board turnover is expensive in terms of recruitment, training, and orientation costs. Board members need to serve through their terms (yes, they need terms) completely. But more importantly, a large board turnover can often result in an inability to get anything done due to a lack of quorums. The board needs the quorum required in your bylaws to make any legal decision. Obviously, illegal decisions are not wise.

This problem may indicate poor board leadership (a dominating or unpleasant person who makes the meetings less than fun), haphazard board recruitment (board members aren't told everything that is expected of them), or other problems.

No new programs or methods of mission provision

If you are doing exactly and only the same programs, in the same physical space, in the same time frames, with the same methodology, that you were five years ago, or even two years—you are not innovating, not practicing lifelong learning, not seeking to improve. Even if your programs are wonderful, they can always be better. Even if you are on the cutting edge today, that edge is dulled over time if you do not stay current.

No regular and repeated asking

One of the characteristics of successful organizations we discussed in Chapter 1 was that of a "bias for marketing." Such a bias requires that *everyone* be on the marketing team, and that you try to give people what they need *in ways that they want*. This requires asking. As a warning sign, *not* asking (no surveys, no interviews, no focus groups, and so forth) means that the organization is not innovating, not interested in what people want, only in giving them what they *need*, not lifelong learners and thus not good stewards. Asking is an *essential* part of stewardship.

No budget—one that is ignored— or one that is amended each month

As a steward, you need to develop budgets and then make sure that you monitor their implementation. In budgeting, you look at your strategic plan, review your priorities, look at the funding streams, and make a best estimate of how to match up community needs with the resources you expect to have in hand over the coming twelve months. You agree on what really is a best guess and you move ahead, holding each other accountable. Budgeting is a crucial part of financial oversight, good management, and good stewardship.

How can you do your financial job without doing this task? Yet people trivialize or sabotage the budget process in one of three ways: First, some organizations have *no* budget. Second, there are organizations that have a budget but tend to ignore it—even if reports show it to be way under in income or way over in expenses. In other words, the budget is trivialized. Third, some organizations are determined always to be on budget—a laudable goal, but to get there they amend their budget every quarter, or even every month. This shapes their budget to their income and expenses, rather than the correct way—shaping income and expenses to meet the budget. Sometimes a budget needs to be reviewed and corrected, but too much indicates trouble.

No continuing education for staff or board

A stewardship organization knows that lifelong learning results in innovation, continued excellence, and effective mission provision. And yet many organizations include no line item for training or continuing education, or cut it during tumultuous times. Such cuts directly affect the quality of services in six to eighteen months. Lack of a priority for learning is a sign of trouble.

Out-of-date personnel, financial, or other policies

Having good policies is an important management responsibility. Policies protect your assets, protect your board and staff, give management the ability to manage rather than merely administer day to day. Policies set limits and let people know what is expected of them. A lack of policies, or policies that are far out of date, indicate lack of management focus, and a tendency to *deal with the urgent rather than the important.* Such a tendency is dangerous over both the short and long term.

Little sharing of internal information among staff and board

Internal information, including plans, financial reports, budgets, and draft policies, should be widely shared. This improves ownership, team-work, and the quality of the work done by the organization. Poor sharing of information is always a red flag. As a steward your job is to get the most mission out the door with the resources at hand. One of the most important resources you have is your staff, so why not include them in the learning, knowing, thinking, and problem-solving processes? You can't know it all, no matter how smart you are.

No current strategic plan

As Yogi Berra famously said, "If you don't know where you're going, you'll wind up somewhere else." You can't efficiently and effectively per-form the mission if you are only operating month to month or even year to year. Planning focuses you on your priorities, core competencies, and how you match those competencies with the most pressing needs in your community.

A break-even pattern or consistent money loss

Organizations that only break even every year or, worse, lose money, are at severe risk. While not every service has to make money, the organiza-tion as a whole needs to. An organization that is at best breaking even usually has some concomitant problems: a board that feels that profits are immoral, overdependence on funders whose policies keep the organiza-tion poor (and powerless), or staff who put their hearts way out in front of their heads. Remember, the first rule is "Mission, mission, mission," but the second rule, "No money, no mission," is very, very close behind.

Too much debt

Too much debt is bad for individuals, bad for for-profits, and can be deadly for not-for-profits, particularly if it shows up as a result of a sudden cessation of a profitable funding stream. It is most dangerous if a board or staff is set against making a profit. Why? *Because debt is only paid back by profits.*

No staff or board turnover

Too much turnover is obviously detrimental to the organization, but too *little* turnover is also troubling. If you haven't changed any staff or any board members for three years (and you have more than three staff and five board members), you risk stagnation. New people bring new ideas, new energy, new perspective, new solutions for problems, and new ways to improve. This is not intended to denigrate long-term staff or board. Again, it's a question of balance.

Inadequate marketing materials

Lack of a leadership priority on marketing might take several forms: not asking; not paying attention to marketing materials that are old or of poor quality; not training staff in good customer service techniques. It often indicates either a "we know best" attitude—which is self-destructive in a competitive environment—or, worse, ignorance about this very important area for any mission-based organization. Marketing materials that focus only on the service (the organization) and not on how it solves problems for the market are a clear sign of trouble.

Poor use of technology

Poor use of technology shows up in several ways: some organizations refuse to use new technologies; some rely on poor-quality, donated computers (known in the tech consulting world as "boxes from hell"); some invest money in every new idea, every new gimmick, every new upgrade. Technology is not a panacea—it's a tool. Properly, it should make what you do easier, more efficient, more effective, resulting in improved services. Unfortunately, it can also distract us from provision of service. But most importantly, technology is a fact of our lives. It is ubiquitous in our society and, more importantly, *an expectation of our markets*.

Those are the warning signs of trouble in your organization. Let's hope you didn't see your organization reflected in this list at all—or at least not too often. Keep the list handy so that you can regularly jump on any of these problems if they surface in the future.

Recap

In this chapter, you have learned a lot about your organization and yourself. Two assessments, one for your organization and one for your personal stewardship, helped you develop benchmarks for organizational and personal stewardship. I hope you have taken the time to use them, and thus to begin the process of organizational improvement and self-improvement. If the news was not as good as you wanted, take heart. A wise person once told me this:

> *"Praise feeds the ego. We all need to be told 'good job' when we deserve it. But criticism feeds improvement. The first step in getting better is knowing what's wrong."*

Finally, we looked at warning signs of organizational trouble. To review these, they were:

- No financial information being reported
- Excessive staff turnover
- Excessive board turnover—or lack of quorums
- No new programs or methods of mission provision
- No regular or repeated asking
- No budget—or one that is amended each month—or one that is ignored

- No continuing education for staff or board
- Out-of-date personnel, financial, or other policies
- Little sharing of internal information among staff and board
- No current strategic plan
- A break-even pattern or consistent money loss
- Too much debt
- No staff or board turnover
- Inadequate marketing materials
- Poor use of technology

CHAPTER TEN DISCUSSION QUESTIONS

1. What surprises did we find in the organizational self-assessment? What can we do to enhance the good surprises and fix the bad ones?

2. Were there factors missing from the assessments that are important to us? Should we start measuring them? If so, how and how often?

3. What should we do with this assessment? How far internally should we circulate it?

4. How soon should we take the assessment again?

5. What did people learn about themselves from taking the personal self-assessment?

6. Is there a consensus that we need certain training or continuing education to work on such issues as motivation, innovation, communications skills, or other issues?

7. Are you motivated to be better stewards because of this exercise? Why or why not?

FINAL THOUGHTS

Our journey together through the concepts and suggestions about stewardship is just about done, but your journey to becoming a steward and maintaining a stewardship organization has really just started. Thus, a couple of things before I go.

First, try to keep in mind in all that you do, in every decision you make, the point of your job, the reason you are spending so much of your life in and around your not-for-profit, is the mission and the people that mission touches. You have the true privilege of working in an organization that can, and almost certainly does, touch people's lives for the better. Your organization may heal, teach, inspire, protect, or improve your community in one of many ways, but there is always more to do using the resources with which you have been entrusted.

People who are passionate about their work often describe it as a calling, not just a job. I hope that entering the stewardship mind-set will help you reach that level of commitment and enjoyment in your work. Remember that you are a special person, helping a special organization do work that most other people would never even try.

Good for you. And because of what you do, good for all of us.

Be well, do good mission, and enjoy the challenges and rewards of stewardship.

Peter Brinckerhoff
Springfield, Illinois

RESOURCES

This book is the start of your stewardship journey, but there is always a lot more to learn. The resources listed here will get you started.

One of the most wonderful changes in the field of not-for-profit management over the past two decades has been the constantly expanding set of resources available to not-for-profit boards, employees, volunteers, and funders. That cornucopia of resources leads to a problem: no one can spend twenty-four hours of every day learning. How do you focus on what's important?

Listed here are three or four of the best publications and web sites for each of the topics we touched on in this book. In some cases a resource is listed more than once, since some have multiple applications. Also listed are some general resources that you should check out first. You will also note that while most of the books and web sites are focused on the not-for-profit sector, some are not. Take an extra moment to look at these resources, as they often provide an important and different perspective on problems that may vex you.

The web sites serve mixed purposes. Some are topic-specific; some are organization-specific related to the topic. All are terrific.

Finally, while I have tried to choose the best sites and the best publications, "the best" is a moving target. New print and media resources, new training, and new web sites come out all the time. Therefore, I have a special offer for readers of this book. Check out the section of my own web site particularly developed and set aside just for you: www.mission-based.com/stewardship.htm

There you will see this resource list online with regular updates and links to the posted web sites and books. There is also an option to sign up for my free monthly online newsletter, which touches on management, marketing, technology, and new publications in each issue. And once you are at my web site, you can check the extensive links and publications areas, as well as see management, marketing, and technology tips.

A final note about resources: while books and workbooks are great, go to live trainings too. Printed matter and online libraries are great, but live training allows you to ask questions, interact with other participants, participate in debate, and learn more deeply. Fortunately there is a lot of training around. Keep your eyes open for what your peers are studying. Find out which accessible colleges and universities have programs in not-for-profit management and get on their mailing lists. If you have a community foundation or a management services organization, talk to them about their training efforts. Ask your funders for training venues as well. Then, when you have the information, force yourself (and your staff and board) to carve out the time to go to live training. You'll be glad you did, and the people you serve will benefit.

Happy lifelong learning!

Online Stewardship Resources

The resources listed in this section are updated regularly at the author's web site. To find the newest additions, go to

www.missionbased.com/stewardship.htm

General Resources

Publishers

These are the three largest publishers of not-for profit materials. Call or visit their web sites to get on their catalog mailing lists, or just search for the topic you want on the web site.

Fieldstone Alliance
60 Plato Boulevard East, Suite 150
Saint Paul, MN 55107
Telephone: 800-274-6024; 651-556-4500
www.FieldstoneAlliance.org

John Wiley & Sons
Professional and Trade Division
111 River Street
Hoboken, NJ 07030-5774
Telephone: 800-956-7739
www.wiley.com

Jossey-Bass
989 Market Street
San Francisco, CA 94103-1741
Telephone: 415-433-1740
Fax: 415-433-0499
www.josseybass.com

Web sites

I regularly send client organizations to these general management web sites, since they are so deep and wide and have so much to offer in so many areas.

1. **Free Management Library:** An amazingly in-depth look at more than seventy-five categories of information. Many include short online courses. Mega-kudos to Carter McNamara, who put the site together. www.mapnp.org/library/

2. **Nonprofit FAQ:** Much more than a simple list of frequently asked questions, this site is the best of its kind on the web, thanks to Putnam Barber.

3. **CEO Express:** A site of links to many good pieces of information. Designed primarily for the for-profit world, it is useful for business research and publication information, and there is a set of resources just for not-for-profit managers as well. www.ceoexpress.com

4. **Nonprofit.gov:** At some point you will need information from the government about start-up, filing forms, state registration information, or other federal or state information. It's all gathered and accessible for you here. www.nonprofit.gov

The Mission-Based Management Series

My previous books cover a lot of ground in the area of not-for-profit management. *Mission-Based Management* and *Mission-Based Marketing* are both in their second edition and have associated workbooks. These, as well as *Social Entrepreneurship* and *Faith-Based Management*, are used in a wide number of graduate and undergraduate programs worldwide. All are available through my web site: www.missionbased.com/publications/missionbased.htm

or at John Wiley & Sons' web site: www.wiley.com

Training

Management Support Organizations: Many Management Support Organizations provide a wide array of training to not-for-profits of all shapes and sizes in their communities. For a list of MSOs near you, go to the following web site: www.idealist.org/tools/support-orgs.html

State Nonprofit Associations: State associations also sometimes provide training. The National Council of Nonprofit Associations is a network of nearly forty statewide associations. You can find links to the association in your state, read some case studies, and subscribe to a tax newsletter. www.ncna.org/

Community Foundations: Many sponsor training in not-for-profit management, fund raising, leadership, and other key skills. For a list of community foundations in your area, go to http://lnp.foundationcenter.org/finder.html

College and University Level Training: Check with your local colleges and universities. Programs in not-for-profit management are exploding in number, variety, and focus. For a list from 2001 from Seton Hall, visit http://tltc.shu.edu/npo/

Stewardship

Books

1. Block, Peter. *Stewardship: Choosing Service over Self-Interest.* San Francisco: Berrett-Kohler Publishers, 1993.

2. Blachard, Ken, and Phil Hodges. *Servant Leader: Transforming Your Heart, Head, Hands, & Habits.* Nashville: J. Countryman Books, 2002.

3. Greenleaf, Robert K., Don M. Frick, and Larry C. Spears, editors. *On Becoming a Servant Leader.* San Francisco: Jossey-Bass, 1996.

Web sites

1. **Stewardship Project:** A really interesting site full of research, philosophies, policies, articles, and guidance for a world-wide network of stewards. http://the-stewardship.org/

2. **Alliance for Regional Stewardship:** A network of people who are working for community good, particularly in urban areas of the United States. www.regionalstewardship.org/

3. **Ted Mollegen** has a great site about faith-based stewardship—very ecumenical, with lots of links. http://members.aol.com/stewdship/

Leadership

Books

1. Howe, Fischer. *The Nonprofit Leadership Team: Building the Board-Executive Director Partnership.* San Francisco: Jossey-Bass, 2004.

2. Riggio, Ronald E., and Sarah Smith Orr, editors. *Improving Leadership in Nonprofit Organizations.* San Francisco: Jossey-Bass, 2004.

3. Nanus, Burt, and Steven Dobs. *Leaders Who Make a Difference: Essential Strategies for Meeting the Nonprofit Challenge.* San Francisco: Jossey-Bass, 1999.

Web sites

No specific recommendations (as of this writing) in nonprofit leadership—but to see numerous educational programs on nonprofit leadership, just enter the term into a search engine such as Google.com.

Financial Management

Books

1. Dropkin, Murray, and Bill LaTouche. *The Budget-Building Book for Nonprofits : A Step-By-Step Guide for Nonprofit Managers and Boards.* San Francisco: Jossey-Bass, 1998.

2. Ruppel, Warren. *Not-For-Profit Accounting Made Easy.* New York: John Wiley & Sons, 2002.

3. McGlaughlin, Thomas. *Streetsmart Financial Basics for Nonprofit Managers.* New York: John Wiley & Sons, 2002.

Web sites

1. **Nonprofit Finance Fund:** Helps nonprofits with all kinds of financial advice and assistance. www.nonprofitfinancefund.org/

2. **Nonprofit Financial Center:** Another site for many different kinds of financial assistance and guidance. www.nfconline.org/main/info/faq.htm

3. **Financial Management Resources:** From the Tampa Bay Management Assistance Project—a great listing. www.maptampabay.org/main.asp?ID=54#Financial%20Management

Marketing

Books

1. Herron, Douglas B. *Marketing Nonprofit Programs and Services: Proven and Practical Strategies to Get More Customers, Members, and Donors.* San Francisco: Jossey-Bass, 1997.

2. Andreasen, Alan R., and Philip Kotler. *Strategic Marketing for Nonprofit Organizations,* 6th ed. Upper Saddle River, NJ: Prentice Hall, 2003.

3. Stern, Gary J. *Marketing Workbook for Nonprofit Organizations, Volume 1: Develop the Plan.* Saint Paul, MN: Fieldstone Alliance, 2001.

Web sites

Although there are a zillion marketing web sites for nonprofits, 99.5 percent are for fundraising.

Planning

Books

1. Allison, Michael, and Jude Kay. *Strategic Planning for Nonprofits: A Practical Guide and Workbook*. New York: John Wiley & Sons, 1997.

2. Barry, Bryan W. *Strategic Planning Workbook for Nonprofit Organizations*. Saint Paul, MN: Fieldstone Alliance, 1997.

3. Bryson, John M., and Farnum K. Alston. *Creating and Implementing Your Strategic Plan: A Workbook for Public and Nonprofit Organizations*. San Francisco: Jossey-Bass, 1996.

Web sites

1. **Free Management Library:** This thing never ends, and all of it is good. The planning portion is at www.managementhelp.org/plan_dec/str_plan/str_plan.htm

2. **Planning Assessment:** A good strategic planning tool from Grizzard Consulting: http://nonprofit.grizzard.com/articles.cfm?mode=single&article_id=53

Board of Directors

Books

1. Weisman, Carol, ed. *Secrets of Successful Boards: The Best of the Nonprofit Pro's*. St. Louis: F.E. Robbins Press, 1998.

2. Tweeten, Byron L. *Transformational Boards: A Practical Guide to Engaging Your Board and Embracing Change*. San Francisco: Jossey-Bass, 2002.

3. Zimmerman, Robert M., and Ann W. Lehman. *Boards that Love Fundraising: A How-To Guide for Your Board*. San Francisco: Jossey-Bass, 2004.

Web sites

1. **BoardSource:** The best place on the web for board information, training, and materials written specifically for board members. www.boardsource.org
2. **Free Toolkit for Boards:** part of Carter McNamara's Free Management site:. www.mapnp.org/library/boards/boards.htm
3. **Nonprofit FAQ on Boards:** A great set of questions and answers. www.nonprofits.org/npofaq/keywords/1a.html

Fundraising

Books

1. Greenfield, James M. *Fundraising Fundamentals: A Guide to Annual Giving for Professionals and Volunteers.* New York: John Wiley & Sons, 2002.
2. Rosso, Hank. Hank Rosso's *Achieving Excellence in Fund Raising,* 2nd ed. San Francisco: Jossey-Bass, 2003.
3. Mutz, John, and Katherine Murray. *Fundraising for Dummies.* Foster City, CA: IDG Books Worldwide, 2000.

Web sites

1. **Fundraising Resources on the Internet:** a great place to start. Provided by the Association of Gospel Rescue Missions, it provides links to all kinds of development resources for both faith-based and secular organizations. www.agrm.org/dev-trak/links.html

INDEX

Notes
c indicates chart
d indicates diagram

More results-oriented books from Fieldstone Alliance

Management

The Accidental Techie
Supporting, Managing, and Maximizing Your Nonprofit's Technology
by Sue Bennett

How to support and manage technology on a day-to-day basis including setting up a help desk, developing a technology budget, working with consultants, handling security, creating a backup system, purchasing hardware and software, using donated hardware, creating a useful database, and more.

176 pages, softcover Item # 069490

Benchmarking for Nonprofits
How to Measure, Manage, and Improve Results
by Jason Saul

This book defines a systematic and reliable way to benchmark (the ongoing process of measuring your organization against leaders)—from preparing your organization to measuring performance and implementing best practices.

128 pages, softcover Item # 069431

The Best of the Board Café
Hands-on Solutions for Nonprofit Boards
by Jan Masaoka, CompassPoint Nonprofit Services

Gathers the most requested articles from the e-newsletter, *Board Café*. You'll find a lively menu of ideas, information, opinions, news, and resources to help board members give and get the most out of their board service.

232 pages, softcover Item # 069407

The Fieldstone Alliance Nonprofit Field Guide to Conducting Successful Focus Groups
by Judith Sharken Simon

Shows how to collect valuable information without a lot of money or special expertise. Using this proven technique, you'll get essential opinions and feedback to help you check out your assumptions, do better strategic planning, improve services or products, and more.

80 pages, softcover Item # 069199

Consulting with Nonprofits:
A Practitioner's Guide
by Carol A. Lukas

A step-by-step, comprehensive guide for consultants. Addresses the art of consulting, how to run your business, and much more. Also includes tips and anecdotes from thirty skilled consultants.

240 pages, softcover Item # 069172

The Fieldstone Alliance Nonprofit Field Guide to Crafting Effective Mission and Vision Statements
by Emil Angelica

Guides you through two six-step processes that result in a mission statement, vision statement, or both. Shows how a clarified mission and vision lead to more effective leadership, decisions, fundraising, and management. Includes tips, sample statements, and worksheets.

88 pages, softcover Item # 06927X

The Fieldstone Alliance Nonprofit Field Guide to Developing Effective Teams
by Beth Gilbertsen and Vijit Ramchandani

Helps you understand, start, and maintain a team. Provides tools and techniques for writing a mission statement, setting goals, conducting effective meetings, creating ground rules to manage team dynamics, making decisions in teams, creating project plans, and developing team spirit.

80 pages, softcover Item # 069202

The Five Life Stages of Nonprofit Organizations
Where You Are, Where You're Going, and What to Expect When You Get There
by Judith Sharken Simon with J. Terence Donovan

Shows you what's "normal" for each development stage which helps you plan for transitions, stay on track, and avoid unnecessary struggles. Includes The Life Stage Assessment to plot your organization's progress in seven arenas of organization development.

128 pages, softcover Item # 069229

For a current list of books and prices, visit www.FieldstoneAlliance.org

The Lobbying and Advocacy Handbook for Nonprofit Organizations
Shaping Public Policy at the State and Local Level
by Marcia Avner

A planning guide and resource for nonprofit organizations that want to influence issues that matter to them. This book will help you decide whether to lobby and then put plans in place to make it work.

240 pages, softcover Item # 069261

The Manager's Guide to Program Evaluation:
Planning, Contracting, and Managing for Useful Results
by Paul W. Mattessich, PhD

Explains how to plan and manage an evaluation that will help identify your organization's successes, share information with key audiences, and improve services.

96 pages, softcover Item # 069385

Marketing Workbook for Nonprofit Organizations Volume I: Develop the Plan
by Gary J. Stern

Don't just wish for results—get them! Here's how to create a straightforward, usable marketing plan. Includes the six Ps of Marketing, how to use them effectively, a sample marketing plan, tips on using the Internet, and worksheets.

208 pages, softcover Item # 069253

Marketing Workbook for Nonprofit Organizations Volume II: Mobilize People for Marketing Success
by Gary J. Stern

Put together a successful promotional campaign based on the most persuasive tool of all: personal contact. Learn how to mobilize your entire organization, its staff, volunteers, and supporters in a focused, one-to-one marketing campaign. Comes with *Pocket Guide for Marketing Representatives.* In it, your marketing representatives can record key campaign messages and find motivational reminders.

192 pages, softcover Item # 069105

The Nonprofit Board Member's Guide to Lobbying and Advocacy
by Marcia Avner

Written specifically for board members, this guide helps organizations increase their impact on policy decisions. It reveals how board members can be involved in planning for and implementing successful lobbying efforts.

96 pages, softcover Item # 069393

The Nonprofit Mergers Workbook
The Leader's Guide to Considering, Negotiating, and Executing a Merger
by David La Piana

Save time, money, and untold frustration with this highly practical guide that makes the process of negotiating a merger manageable and controllable. Includes case studies, decision trees, worksheets, tips, and step-by-step guidance from seeking partners to writing the merger agreement, and more.

240 pages, softcover Item # 069210

The Nonprofit Mergers Workbook Part II
Unifying the Organization after a Merger
by La Piana Associates

Once the merger agreement is signed, the question becomes: How do we make this merger work? *Part II* helps you create a comprehensive plan to achieve *integration*—bringing together people, programs, processes, and systems from two (or more) organizations into a single, unified whole.

248 pages, includes CD-ROM Item # 069415

Resolving Conflict in Nonprofit Organizations
The Leader's Guide to Finding Constructive Solutions
by Marion Peters Angelica

Helps you identify conflict, decide whether to intervene, uncover and deal with the true issues, and design and conduct a conflict resolution process. Includes exercises to learn and practice conflict resolution skills, guidance on handling unique conflicts such as harassment and discrimination, and when (and where) to seek outside help with litigation, arbitration, and mediation.

192 pages, softcover Item # 069164

Strategic Planning Workbook for Nonprofit Organizations, Revised and Updated
by Bryan Barry

Chart a wise course for your nonprofit's future. This time-tested workbook gives you practical step-by-step guidance, real-life examples, one nonprofit's complete strategic plan, and easy-to-use worksheets.

144 pages, softcover Item # 069075

Finance

Bookkeeping Basics
What Every Nonprofit Bookkeeper Needs to Know
by Debra L. Ruegg and Lisa M. Venkatrathnam
Complete with step-by-step instructions, a glossary of accounting terms, detailed examples, and reproducible forms, this book will enable you to meet the basic bookkeeping requirements of your nonprofit organization.
128 pages, softcover Item # 069296

Coping with Cutbacks
The Nonprofit Guide to Success When Times Are Tight
by Emil Angelica and Vincent Hyman
Shows you practical ways to involve business, government, and other nonprofits to solve problems together. Includes 185 cutback strategies you can put to use right away.
128 pages, softcover   Item # 069091

Financial Leadership for Nonprofit Executives
Guiding Your Organization to Long-term Success
by Jeanne Peters and Elizabeth Schaffer
Provides executives with a practical guide to protecting and growing the assets of their organizations and with accomplishing as much mission as possible with those resources.
144 pages, softcover Item # 06944X

Venture Forth! The Essential Guide to Starting a Moneymaking Business in Your Nonprofit Organization
by Rolfe Larson
The most complete guide on nonprofit business development. Building on the experience of dozens of organizations, this handbook gives you a time-tested approach for finding, testing, and launching a successful nonprofit business venture.
272 pages, softcover Item # 069245

Collaboration

Collaboration Handbook
Creating, Sustaining, and Enjoying the Journey
by Michael Winer and Karen Ray
Shows you how to get a collaboration going, set goals, determine everyone's roles, create an action plan, and evaluate the results. Includes a case study of one collaboration from start to finish, helpful tips on how to avoid pitfalls, and worksheets to keep everyone on track.
192 pages, softcover Item # 069032

Collaboration: What Makes It Work, 2nd Ed.
by Paul Mattessich, PhD, Marta Murray-Close, BA, and Barbara Monsey, MPH
An in-depth review of collaboration research. Twenty key factors influencing successful collaborations are identified. Includes The Wilder Collaboration Factors Inventory, which groups can use to assess their collaboration.
104 pages, softcover Item # 069326

A Fieldstone Alliance Nonprofit Guide to Forming Alliances
by Linda Hoskins and Emil Angelica
Helps you understand the wide range of ways that they can work with others—focusing on alliances that work at a lower level of intensity. It shows how to plan and start an alliance that fits a nonprofit's circumstances and needs.
112 pages, softcover Item # 069466

The Nimble Collaboration
Fine-Tuning Your Collaboration for Lasting Success
by Karen Ray
Shows you ways to make your existing collaboration more responsive, flexible, and productive. Provides three key strategies to help your collaboration respond quickly to changing environments and participants.
136 pages, softcover Item # 069288

Funder's Guides

Community Visions, Community Solutions
Grantmaking for Comprehensive Impact
by Joseph A. Connor and Stephanie Kadel-Taras
128 pages, softcover Item # 06930X

A Funder's Guide to Evaluation: Leveraging Evaluation to Improve Nonprofit Effectiveness
by Peter York
160 pages, softcover Item # 069482

A Funder's Guide to Organizational Assessment: Tools, Processes, and Their Use in Building Capacity
by GEO
216 pages, CD-ROM included   Item # 069539

Strengthening Nonprofit Performance
A Funder's Guide to Capacity Building
by Paul Connolly and Carol Lukas
176 pages, softcover Item # 069377

For a current list of books and prices, visit www.FieldstoneAlliance.org

Vital Communities

Community Building: What Makes It Work
by Wilder Research Center
112 pages, softcover Item # 069121

Community Economic Development Handbook
Strategies and Tools to Revitalize Your
Neighborhood
by Mihailo Temali
288 pages, softcover Item # 069369

The Community Leadership Handbook
Framing Ideas, Building Relationships, and
Mobilizing Resources
by Jim Krile
240 pages, softcover Item # 069547

The Fieldstone Alliance Nonprofit Field Guide to
Conducting Community Forums
by Carol Lukas and Linda Hoskins
128 pages, softcover Item # 069318

The Creative Community Builder's Handbook
How to Transform Communities Using Local Assets,
Art, and Culture
by Thomas Borrup
272 pages, softcover Item # 069474

New Americans, New Promise
A Guide to the Refugee Journey in America
by Yorn Yan
200 pages, softcover Item # 069504

ORDERING INFORMATION

Order by phone, fax or online

 Call toll-free: 800-274-6024
Internationally: 651-556-4509

 Fax: 651-556-4517

 E-mail: books@fieldstonealliance.org
Online: www.FieldstoneAlliance.org

Mail: Fieldstone Alliance
Publishing Center
60 Plato BLVD E, STE 150
St. Paul, MN 55107

Our NO-RISK guarantee

If you aren't completely satisfied with any book for
any reason, simply send it back within 30 days for
a full refund.

Pricing and discounts

For current prices and discounts, please visit our
web site at www.FieldstoneAlliance.org or call toll
free at 800-274-6024.

Do you have a book idea?

Fieldstone Alliance seeks manuscripts and
proposals for books in the fields of nonprofit management and community development. To get a copy of
our author guidelines, please call us at 800-274-6024.
You can also download them from our web site at
www.FieldstoneAlliance.org.

Visit us online

You'll find information about Fieldstone Alliance
and more details on our books, such as table of contents, pricing, discounts, endorsements, and more, at
www.FieldstoneAlliance.org

Quality assurance

We strive to make sure that all the books we publish
are helpful and easy to use. Our major workbooks are
tested and critiqued by experts before being published.
Their comments help shape the final book and—we
trust—make it more useful to you.